Critical
Essays
in
Modern
Literature

Richard Wright

RUSSELL CARL BRIGNANO

Richard Wright

An Introduction
to the Man
and His Works

UNIVERSITY OF PITTSBURGH PRESS

Grateful acknowledgment is made to the following for permission to quote material that appears in this book:

Harper & Row, Publishers, Inc., for quotations from *Black Boy: A Record of Childhood and Youth,* by Richard Wright. Copyright, 1937, 1942, 1944, 1945, by Richard Wright. For quotations from *Black Power: A Record of Reactions in a Land of Pathos,* by Richard Wright. Copyright, 1954, by Richard Wright. For quotations from *How "Bigger" Was Born: The Story of Native Son, One of the Most Significant Novels of Our Times, and How It Came to Be Written,* by Richard Wright. Copyright, 1940, by Richard Wright. For quotations from *Native Son,* by Richard Wright. Copyright, 1940, by Richard Wright. For quotations from *The Outsider,* by Richard Wright. Copyright, 1953, by Richard Wright. For quotations from *Uncle Tom's Children: Four Novellas,* by Richard Wright. Copyright, 1936, 1938, by Richard Wright. And for quotations from Richard Wright's essay in *The God That Failed,* edited by Richard Crossman. Copyright, 1944, by Richard Wright.

Paul R. Reynolds, Inc., for quotations from *Pagan Spain,* by Richard Wright. Copyright © 1957 by Richard Wright. For quotations from *12 Million Black Voices: A Folk History of the Negro in the United States,* by Richard Wright. Copyright 1941 by Richard Wright. For quotations from "I Bite the Hand That Feeds Me," by Richard Wright, in *Atlantic Monthly,* June 1940. Copyright 1940, by The Atlantic Monthly Company, Boston, Mass. For quotations from "Blueprint for Negro Writing," by Richard Wright, in *The New Challenge,* Fall 1937. And for quotations from *Savage Holiday,* by Richard Wright. Copyright © 1954, by Richard Wright. All reprinted by permission from Paul R. Reynolds, Inc., 599 Fifth Avenue, New York, N.Y. 10017.

International Publishers Co. Inc., for quotations from *Bright and Morning Star,* by Richard Wright. Reprinted by permission of International Publishers Co. Inc. Copyright © 1941.

Doubleday & Company, Inc., for quotations from *The Long Dream,* by Richard Wright. Copyright © 1958 by Richard Wright. And for quotations from *White Man, Listen!* by Richard Wright. Copyright © 1957 by Richard Wright. Both reprinted by permission of Doubleday & Company, Inc.

Avon Books, for quotations from *Lawd Today.* Copyright © 1963 by Ellen Wright, reprinted from *Lawd Today,* by Richard Wright, by permission of Avon Books.

The World Publishing Company, for quotations from *The Color Curtain: A Report on the Bandung Conference,* by Richard Wright. Copyright © 1956 by Richard Wright. And for quotations from *Eight Men,* by Richard Wright. Copyright, ©, 1961, 1940, by Richard Wright. "The Man Who Lived Underground" was originally published by L. B. Fischer Corp. Copyright, ©, 1944 by L. B. Fischer Corp.

The John Day Company, Inc., for quotations from *The New World of Negro Americans.* Copyright © 1963 by Massachusetts Institute of Technology. Reprinted from *The New World of Negro Americans,* by Harold R. Isaacs, by permission of The John Day Company, Inc., publisher.

G. P. Putnam's Sons, for quotations from *Richard Wright: A Biography,* by Constance Webb. Copyright © 1968 by Constance Webb.

Beacon Press, Inc., for quotations from *Notes of a Native Son,* by James Baldwin. © 1955 by James Baldwin.

Contents

Preface : ix

Acknowledgments : xiii

1 On the American Primary Colors : 3

2 Marxism, the Party, and a Negro Writer : 50

3 New Perspectives Outside America : 87

4 The Philosophical Premises : 120

5 New Directions? A Postscript : 166

Notes : 173

Selected Bibliography : 191

Index : 199

Preface

RICHARD NATHANIEL WRIGHT was born near Natchez, Mississippi, in 1908. His life represented, among other things, a search to discover whether black men could live with dignity and without fear in a world dominated by white men. His early concerns centered upon race relations in the United States. As the perimeter of his experiences broadened beyond the American South, beyond America too, he quested for answers to problems even greater than those associated with American race relations, although the initial thrust of his search was never abandoned. In his later years Wright settled in France in a self-imposed exile from his native land, traveling periodically to other countries and continents. He died unexpectedly from natural causes at Paris in 1960.

Wright is best remembered for his works dealing with twentieth-century Negro-white relations, especially for his autobiographical *Black Boy* (1945) and for *Native Son* (1940), a novel. Anyone aspiring to comprehend the ways in which many Negroes have lived in and responded to their America during this century will be well rewarded from consulting much of Wright's work. In so doing and in reading the creative literature of other Negroes, he will also learn that *Native Son* occupies a special place among American letters. The popular success of that novel marks a turning point in the history of Negro writing. Perhaps, too, *The Outsider* (1953), a novel consciously inspired by existential materials, will be studied more carefully and often as a major example of Western philosophical fiction. A lengthy short story "The Man Who Lived Underground" (1944) will continue to make its way into many anthologies. Hopefully, the artistic skills behind the stories collected in *Uncle Tom's Children* (1938) will always be appreciated. From the standpoint of language, narration, and theme, they represent Wright the artist at his best.

Wright was neither a consistent, refined craftsman nor a stylistic innovator. His successes are colossal, his failures dreadful. His creative efforts usually reveal first a Negro conscious of his race, second an artist committed to polished performance. However, he is a fascinating figure not only for literary critics, but also for historians, sociologists, and philosophers. He was actively immersed within many of the major social and intellectual movements of the first half of the twentieth century, and much of his fiction and nonfiction was focused upon them. The rise of science, the ramifications of industrialism, the effects of Marxism, the emergence in world politics of new power configurations composed of ex-colonial peoples, the growth of secularism, the development of modern philosophies of existence—all are treated by Wright in his diverse works. The limited vision of a poorly educated black boy in the white man's American South grew to encompass the currents of the history of his time.

This study of Wright combines literary criticism, biography, and historical matter. The nature of his publications offers little alternative. To have devoted attention only to a critical analysis of his literary works would have been to squander energy on much that is aesthetically displeasing and thus not worth close critical appraisal. To have excluded a historical perspective would have been to disregard irresponsibly the pertinent relationships among the author's life, his environment, and his publications. To have eliminated biography entirely would have been to overlook much in Wright's books that is autobiographical.

Wright's paramount public concerns can be isolated into four areas: race relations in America, Marxism, contemporary international affairs, and Wright's own changing philosophical props. Each of these concerns has been assigned a chapter. A brief final chapter deals with scattered pieces and fragments written by Wright during his last three or four years.

In critical studies such as this it is tempting to divide the book into distinct chronological time periods; however, the overlapping thematic material in Wright's writings is too extensive to make such a structure practical. For example, Wright was concerned with American racial problems as much in *The Long Dream* (1958) as in *Native Son*, written nearly two decades earlier; and although Marxism and the Communist Party captured his imagination and helped to inform his works in one way or another roughly from 1932 to 1942, they intrude appreciably and pointedly in *The Outsider* and in his nonfiction of the 1950s. Thus, for example, in Chapter 1 the racial theme of *Native Son* is discussed, but the Marxist and existential philosophical materials of that novel are withheld for treatment in subsequent chapters. Repetition and confusion have been minimized by the use of appropriate brief recapitulations and occasional cross-references from chapter to chapter. The inclusion of plot information will, hopefully, give a reader not familiar with all Wright's publications a discernible outline of the works.

A generalization applicable to Wright and his works will

become increasingly apparent in this study. It is an expansion of remarks written randomly by Harold R. Isaacs and John A. Williams. The first understood Wright to be an intellectual who "clung hard to the idea of some larger commonwealth for human society than the tribe, the nation, or the race."[1] The second offered a summary for Wright's publications: "One thought pervaded all of Wright's work: that the perennial human failing—man's gross inhumanity to man—had to be abolished."[2] An additional contention is that, despite Wright's personal agony and outrage stemming from the very fact of his black skin color in a white-dominated Western culture, his fundamental belief was that inhumanity could be abolished if man would heed his reason.

Acknowledgments

HELPING TO GUIDE ME through my early explorations of Richard Wright's works was Professor Walter B. Rideout of the University of Wisconsin, to whom I owe special thanks. A Vilas Fellowship from the estate of William F. Vilas gave me precious time and freedom during a graduate year at Wisconsin to explore the Wright materials that I would later use in this book. A Maurice Falk Foundation summer grant, awarded through the College of Humanities and Social Sciences of Carnegie-Mellon University, provided me an uninterrupted and unimpeded period to continue my research and then to begin writing. I am also indebted to the many helpful and gracious people at the Memorial Library of the University of Wisconsin, the New York City Library, the Hillman Library of the University of Pittsburgh, and the Hunt Library of Carnegie-Mellon University. My gratitude is also extended to Louise Craft, who gave my manuscript its final reading.

Richard Wright

CHAPTER 1

On the American
Primary Colors

RICHARD WRIGHT'S JOURNEY outward from the American South to the rest of the world began in 1927, when he departed Memphis for Chicago. Though perhaps he did not know it at the time, the most prominent baggage he carried was something he could never misplace or lose—the color of his skin. The fact that he was a Negro would intrude upon the very mode of his existence and would influence the direction of his thought, and most certainly later did inform the bulk of his public writing. Through succeeding geographical wanderings, Wright was transported to such scattered points as Spain, Indonesia, Argentina, and the African Gold Coast. However, he was inevitably returned to the attitudes about American racial matters that were fostered within him during his childhood and adolescence.

Wright's flight from the South—from the locale of his early experiences—was intended by him to be a quest to "learn who I was, what I might be." The educational, often-painful peregrinations that followed only accentuated the young Negro's suspicion that "I could never really leave the South, for my feelings had already been formed by the South, for there had been slowly instilled into my

3

personality and consciousness . . . the culture of the South."[1] However, American Southern culture framed Wright not in the posture of a submissive Negro. Rather, he stood firm in attacking any acceptance of an imposed servile stance. Wright questioned the nature of the American society around him, whether it functioned in the South or in the North; and he demanded justifications for, or alterations within, that society. His own focus on racial problems in America usually created an image of the two worlds of his childhood experience, one black, the other white and hostile. The image often became blurred by the intensity of his own anger, which was inflamed by a sense of his being treated unjustly as a Negro in a land promising so much justice for everyone.

Wright's responses were not always patently predictable. Exceptions most often appeared when he described Negroes and whites in Northern urban settings and while, for a decade or so, he was subscribing to optimistic hopes based upon his belief in Marxism. Nevertheless, when his works are concerned with American racial topics, their tone is one of strong protest, as most readers and critics quickly note. Wright's first-published novel (but not the first he wrote), *Native Son*, remains the epitome of American-Negro protest fiction. However, the authorial outlook, the tone, and the subject matter permeating *Native Son* and many of Wright's later pieces have their foundations in the autobiography of Wright's youth, *Black Boy*, and an earlier short companion piece, "The Ethics of Living Jim Crow" (1937). For ascending to an overview of Wright—both the man and the public writer— *Black Boy* is a key document.

A chronicle of fear, frustration, and inner rage, *Black Boy* is a personal account of Wright's pre-Northern and pre-Marxist days. It is ostensibly an autobiography of chronological events and derives its impact from Wright's constant revelations of his emotional and intellectual responses to encounters with social practices and individuals. Each word seems charged with an urgent and immediate quality. The reason soon becomes clear: whereas *Black Boy* is an anger-filled reaction to American society, it is also a sensitive quest for self-discovery. The search for a respectable and safe place in American society for Wright —for Negroes in general—is accompanied by a painful need for both a vocation and a father. In this latter respect the authorial voice in *Black Boy* has been compared to the narrative voices in some of James Joyce's works.[2] In a tragic way the discoveries made by the young Wright were more upsetting and shattering than those which often burst forth into the consciousness of a Stephen Daedalus–Hero–Joyce figure. Wright did learn that his vocational calling came from the domain of art. He also perceived that he was a Negro—not quite an American, not even quite a human being. *Black Boy* does conclude on a hopeful note: Wright would seek a home and his manhood in what he thought would be a more amicable environment, the American North. Nevertheless, his guarded optimism had already been undercut by a failure to find satisfaction and fulfillment in racial togetherness and familial intimacy in the South.

Penetrating deeply into the needs of an individual personality, *Black Boy* thus acquires a universal appeal. However, helpful in explaining specifically the themes, settings, and characters are the narrower concerns of the autobiography. In this respect Rebecca C. Barton has offered an incisive observation in asserting that in *Black Boy*, Wright is "the most genuine representative of lower-class life and in the best position to portray its hunger, its misery, its despair."[3] Actually, the dividing line between what emanates from a life in poverty and a life in America as a

Negro, especially in the South, is generally an obscure one; and much current sociological research has been devoted to locating that line and to determining, in fact, whether there is a division or, instead, an equation. In *Black Boy*, Wright blends an undertone of potential strife and violence between the white and black races with the poverty and personal conflicts within his family to produce a dominant tone of anger against white men. For instance, Wright's search for a father was a real one. His father apparently was an unrelenting tyrant who eventually ran off with another woman. He left behind to survive in rural Mississippi an already indigent family and an ill wife. The ensuing years of physical hunger, of hard work at various jobs, of deprivation of a formal education—all compounded within a social structure separating its members according to skin color—could no doubt have caused responses to race relations that really had had their sources in the individual family problems and family economic position. Yet, in *Black Boy*, precisely what Wright tries to accomplish is a fusion of the particular with the general: the story of one Negro and his family is projected into a tale of all Negroes of the South.[4] Negro poverty and family frictions are transformed into circumstances growing out of the general social structure. The search for a father becomes a search for Negro dignity, economic opportunity, and social acceptance in a racially integrated South, so that the father figure might be respected as a man in the world and so that a Richard Wright might not be compelled to confess bitterly, "If someone had suggested that my father be killed, I would perhaps have become interested."[5]

Autobiographies often provoke psychological analyses of their writers. One fascinating critical excursion into the psyche behind *Black Boy* has been offered by Ralph K. White.[6] From a study of Wright's autobiography, he attempts a summary of Wright's personality traits. He does not answer the question of to what extent Wright's experiences within his family affected his attitudes toward race relations. However, he does identify those characteristics of Wright which seem to intrude upon Wright's treatment of themes in many of his works. White discerns, for example, a high frustration-satisfaction ratio, a tendency to be aggressive and to disapprove of others, a direction of aggressions toward Southern whites, an emphasis on physical safety and security, a doubtful identification with other Negroes, and a stereotyping of adult and white authority.[7] Wright is also credited with "a ruthless honesty of thinking."[8] Conceivably, all these personality characteristics might have originated in isolated experiences within his family. However, as Wright dramatizes in *Black Boy*, their origins are related to a general state of the Negro mind bound up in the daily degradations forcefully proffered by a white-controlled Southern culture. As *Black Boy* progresses, as the Richard Wright encountered in its pages matures, our understanding of his Negro-ness and of his own recognition of an encircling and threatening white Southern society is enlarged. The subject of the autobiography becomes not merely the writer or his family or his particular experiences, but the unfair interplay between white men and black men in the South.

No matter what interpretations of Wright's personality result from a process of easy detection or intense scrutiny and no matter how significant a delineation of the author as constructed from *Black Boy* is to our understanding of his other works, Wright's autobiography stands as an impressive social document. It also may be appreciated for its artistic merits: such fictional devices as dramatic dialogue, vivid physical description, images, symbols, and alliterative language are used effectively and often gracefully by Wright, who by 1945 had become an experienced short-story writer and novelist. The opening lines contain controlling images that form a fitting prelude to most of the content that follows. Describing a day in his fourth year, Wright says, "I crossed restlessly to the window and pushed back the long fluffy white curtains—which I had been forbidden to touch—and looked yearningly out into the empty street."[9] This restlessness of youth is emphasized throughout the work. The street operates as a symbolic barrier dividing different worlds. It additionally functions as a symbolic path of flight, first from one Southern town to another and finally to the North. As the youthful Wright continually tries to push aside the alluring white curtains, a lesson is eventually gained: the Southern whites have established severe penalties for a black man's venturing beyond the curtains. A Negro may approach them if he dares; but for his own survival, he should turn back. The young Wright of *Black Boy* tends to be curious and bold. He often infiltrates beyond the curtains, discovering in time the perils on the other side; but he also develops a contempt for Negroes who remain behind, for Negroes who do not risk. The personal tragedy for Wright, and for the Southern Negro collectively, is that he must leave the South or endanger his life if his boldness is to take him past the curtains.

Wright tells us in *Black Boy* that his initial awareness of the existence of separate black and white worlds occurred in a color vacuum. Although he knew as a child that there were people called whites, he felt no innate emotional response to them. He did sense something different, for he never associated with light-skinned people except for those among his relatives who looked white. However, a train trip from Mississippi to Arkansas soon alerted him to "Jim Crow" practices and instilled in him, "with a sharp concreteness that would never die," the knowledge of two distinct races.[10] A short time later Wright's uncle was killed by a white Arkansas mob, and Wright and his family fled the town. The Negro boy had learned at firsthand what the whites will and can do to black men they feel threatened by. Either through experience or through sad and tragic tales told to him by other Negroes, Wright, as he grew up, collected information and formed impressions about the ways in which contacts between the two races contained hidden and real dangers. Even white children were to be placed on the other side of the race curtain. Encounters with them were confined to rock-throwing skirmishes near a railroad roundhouse that physically divided the two worlds. The youthful Wright began to perceive whites not as real persons but as parts of a general, abhorrent, and potentially destructive force.

The effects of such a seemingly senseless social structure were profound for Wright. His entire being was challenged by the hate and the threats stemming from what, by now, had become a group of almost unreal people, of "invisible whites." Although actually never physically abused by them, the young Wright was "as conditioned to their existence as though I had been the victim of a thousand lynchings."[11] He dreamed of his own vindictive heroics against whites during fantasies of black-initiated racial mob violence; however, no real personal contacts of this nature with whites were ever established to diminish or intensify these fantasies. Wright's imagination helped to create an environment both terrible and strangely remote—as he explains, "something whose horror and blood might descend upon me at any moment."[12]

Wright's vision of a hostile Southern white culture was strengthened even more in time. Support came from his observations during various job experiences in Jackson, Mississippi, and Memphis during the early and mid-1920s. He began to see the manner in which Negro labor was exploited. Not only did he feel that ignorance was being forced upon Negro workers, but he discovered the ways in which a Negro must hide his sense of outrage behind a facade of cheerful subservience in order to remain employed even at menial tasks. Appearance and reality were not merely themes for literary fiction; for the Negro they were real elements in a game surrounded by daily abasement and latent violence. Choices in the game were limited among Negroes, for the whites could always hold out the threat of injury or death and could often find allies among white lawmen. Wright saw the Southern Negro acting out a role assigned to him by the whites, in time even repressing the realization that his life was stunted. The Negro thus had to develop "a delicate, sensitive controlling mechanism" that shut off his mind and emotions "from all that the white race said was taboo."[13] A normal life in the society was replaced by devious and subversive activities. Ways and means were found to cheat white men behind their backs, to gain triumphs great in black men's eyes but hardly noticed as victories by the whites. For example, a teen-aged Wright engaged himself in such illegal activities as stealing money from his employer in a movie box office and bootlegging liquor into a hotel where he worked as a bellboy. Through such actions the Negro ironically reinforced the white man's preconception that he was immoral and prone to crime. His deeds were, in fact, subdued reactions to, and meager consolations for, the repressions forced upon him by the whites.

In *Black Boy* Wright defines a sensitive Negro as one who should not consume a lifetime playing in a consolatory contest of deceit against whites. By engaging in illicit affairs no society admires, he would be preventing his honest impulses from surging into the open—even if such a course should confront the white South with hate and retaliatory violence. Although Wright fully understood the influence of the menaces constantly discouraging the Negro from active and open rebellion, *Black Boy* reveals Wright's ambivalence toward Negroes in general, perhaps partially because of their passivity. With obvious hatred he condemns poor Negroes he happened to see in the Mississippi Delta country. He calls them "a bare, bleak pool of black life," but he also recognizes as his own "our negative confusions, our flights, our fears, our frenzy under pressure."[14] The tragedy and irony for Wright is that he could suggest the need and desire for rebellion, but for himself he found flight imperative.

The message in *Black Boy* is thus divided among the following: a serious presentation of the economic and cultural paucity of Southern Negro life; a call to resistance or rebellion on the part of the Negroes; a plea for white-inspired change; and, finally, personal escape. Although Wright never plainly states that the South would eventually resolve its racial problems, by implication his autobiography speaks toward his limited hope and trust that the ways of the South would be changed, by whites or Negroes or both. Yet, Wright could offer no plan for action. Instead, he fled to Chicago, where his own personality might "grow differently, . . . drink of new and cool rains, bend in strange winds, respond to the warmth of other suns, and, perhaps . . . bloom."[15] Wright's search for Negro dignity and expression, which began when as a child he threw back the white curtains he had been forbidden to touch, could not be concluded in the South. As *Black Boy* so lucidly discloses, what Wright took with him from the South was a pent-up anger and a muffled despair that he would later discharge publicly.

Many of the scenes in *Black Boy* are duplicated from "The Ethics of Living Jim Crow," published earlier, which really is a condensed version of the autobiography in terms of Southern Negro-white racial materials.[16] Wright outlines the differences in physical appearances between white and black neighborhoods in a small Arkansas town. The dirty cinders of the landscape in the Negro area near the railroad tracks are contrasted with the green lawns, hedges, and tree-lined streets in the white areas. These white neighborhoods had become symbols of fear for the young Wright because of his experiences near and in them. For no apparent logical reasons, he felt physically threatened every time he had to enter a white area.

"The Ethics of Living Jim Crow" underscores white intimidation. It also describes some of the methods through which white ascendency is maintained. For instance, as Wright learned while in apprenticeship with a Jackson, Mississippi, optical firm, pressures are put upon the Negro to remain on jobs that are merely menial in nature. Thus, when Wright decided that he was capable of acquiring advanced skills to compete with white labor, he discovered that the white workers had formed a conspiracy against him. After threats had been made upon his life, he was forced to leave and then to look for other menial tasks. Furthermore, he was met with the reactionary ideas of his black kin and friends, who told him he should not aspire to a higher station. If he wanted to work in the South, he should stay in his place. The older heads of the Negro community imparted to him the wisdom of the years—a wisdom based upon a submission to a history of white prejudices and violent acts.

Though a short piece, "The Ethics of Living Jim Crow" also treats the apparent white myth that the Negro male's sexual prowess must be matched or outdone by white virility, and that white women must be protected from the animal instincts of black men. Through this myth, white men find another means to flaunt their overall dominance by molesting Negro women and then expecting Negro men to make no complaints. Any black man's attempt to defend black womanhood is, of course, a sign of general rebellion and must be punished. If a black man is suspected of having had sexual relations with a white woman, he must face castration, if not death, at the hands of a white mob. So Wright recognizes the sexual underpinnings for much that has determined Negro-white relations in the South, and he impartially places them next to other irrational or mythical conditions. However, they are merely a single facet of a whole culture that must be altered.

Both exposition and protest, "The Ethics of Living Jim Crow" reveals some of the reasons why the young Wright felt trapped in the South and why he thus should flee to the North. As protest in particular, it seems to have evolved from a belief—albeit a muted one—that remonstrances might foster significant change. In any event, they would certainly increase within the Negro a sense of dignity and pride that Wright saw so diminished in the South.

The South described in *Black Boy* and in "The Ethics of Living Jim Crow" provides the settings for the short stories published by Wright in the 1930s.[17] Written while he lived in Chicago, they focus upon many of the same Southern racial issues and conflicts that later were to dominate *Black Boy*. Wright also attempts to imitate in dialogues the speech patterns and dialects of Southern Negroes and whites. Playing a significant role in some of the stories are the Great Depression and the resultant social upheaval in America. These influential components of his daily life in Chicago helped to move Wright toward an alliance with the Communist Party through his activities in the John Reed Club. Though Marxist ideology is strong in some of the short stories, it does not overshadow the central focus: the life of ignorance, fear, and shame forced upon the Southern Negro. The Marxist undertones and motifs, especially evident in two of the stories—"Fire and Cloud" and "Bright and Morning Star"—and also noticeable in "Long

Black Song," are considered in Chapter 2. Even in these tales the subject matter revolves primarily around Southern racial problems; however, a Marxist vision does offer an element of hope for the resolution of those problems.

The shortest of Wright's early short stories is "Silt." It is about the hopelessness of a poor Negro tenant farmer, Tom. A victim of a flood that has caused havoc and destruction to his meager crops and equipment, he must somehow feed his wife and child. Although Tom knows that other Negroes are fleeing daily from the clutches of the impoverished land and of the avaricious white landlords, he rides off in the white man Burgess's buggy to beg for money from him to start anew the dismal task of scrub farming. Already substantially in debt to Burgess, Tom increases his own burden and responsibility to the white man. Obviously, the setting and action of the story could easily apply to a white tenant farmer, but Wright intends "Silt" to be a vignette-commentary illustrating Negro acceptance of his poverty. The tone of the story is not consistent: while it creates sympathy for Tom as a victim of nature and of the white man, it also invites the reader to chastise Tom for not moving out, for not seeking a better life. In effect, "Silt" is more a condemnation of a Negro than an outraged attack on the white man. It reflects a fair-mindedness on the part of Wright, for he is willing to include Negro apathy as a vital component of a stagnant, self-perpetuating social and economic condition. Tom becomes a cardboard figure typifying what Wright has all along resented in the Southern Negro psyche—an "Uncle Tom" submissiveness to one's lot.

The theme of escape is treated by Wright in "Big Boy Leaves Home." However, flight here is not premeditated or willful; it is away from imminent danger. The story is replete with violence—the killing of a white man, the tar-and-feathers fiery death of Big Boy's friend Bobo, and the burning of a Negro house by whites. Emphasized is the savagery to which men, both white and black, are propelled because of the curtains of doubt, ignorance, and fear existing among them. Wright also inserts the theme of the Negro as a threat to the white woman, or rather, the Negro as a threat to both the manliness and the sexual prowess of the white male.

The division between the races is portrayed simply and without subtlety through the "No Trespassing" sign enticing four Negro boys to a swimming hole on protected, white-owned property. Young Buck's interpretation of the sign underlies the action and initiates a series of animal images: "Mean ain no dogs n niggers erllowed."[18] The boys innocently frollick in the water in the nude, but a white woman screams at the sight of them. A rescuing white man shoots both Buck and Lester and in turn is killed by Big Boy. The subsequent pursuit of Big Boy and Bobo by the whites is like a hunt for an animal; and Big Boy, driven to find concealment in the damp hole of a deserted kiln, tramples a snake to death. Later, after secretly witnessing Bobo's flaming death, he chokes a barking dog to ensure his own safety. Added to this pattern of savagery is a transformation of the white quest for Negro blood into a frenzied protection of white maidenhood and a defense of white virility. One hunter's remark establishes this theme: "Ef they git erway notta woman in this town would be safe."[19] Big Boy does manage to escape to Chicago, forsaking a land of white sadism. What he had begun in innocence ends in compressed and fearful experience. The story is a miniature reproduction of a nightmarish pattern in *Black Boy*— a youthful and playful incident, followed by white reactions out of all proportion to the alleged offense, followed by flight. Lacking is any semblance of hope for reconciliation between the races in the South. "Big Boy Leaves Home" is thus one example of Wright's most pessimistic and despairing moments.

"Long Black Song" may in some ways be regarded as a companion piece to "Big Boy Leaves Home," for it depicts the fate of a Southern Negro who does not attempt to flee after he has killed a white man. Having discovered that his wife has been seduced by a white traveling salesman, Silas murders him but retreats only as far as his farmhouse to await the arrival of the townsmen he knows will massacre him without trial or jury. He stays on to confront the white posse on his own desparate terms—further revenge at the risk of certain death. He does die fighting, refusing to surrender himself and remaining in his burning house after a furious gun battle with the posse. The action of the story is more than what appears to be a simple plotting of events. Wright portrays Silas as the rural Negro who embraces a version of the American Dream in a doomed effort to win respect in his white-dominated community.[20] Silas has been motivated by his belief in a myth that equates hard work with moneymaking and then with property accumulation, success, and dignity within the community. However, the unfaithfulness of his wife, Sarah, through her sexual relations with a white man finally awakens in Silas the hatred for whites that he has suppressed throughout his quest for success and dignity within the American Dream myth. Wright suggests that the material gains painstakingly made by Silas are futile. Lurking beneath the facade of small empire-building is a truth that Silas at last realizes moments before his death: "The white folks ain never gimme a chance! They ain never give no black man a chance! There ain nothing in yo whole life yuh kin keep from em! They take yo lan! They take yo freedom! They take yo woman! N then they take yo life!"[21] Events in the story do not illustrate all aspects of Silas's assertion, and in this respect "Long Black Song" is not a technically well-wrought piece. However, when the story is read within the context of the other tales in *Uncle Tom's Children*, Silas's claim accumulates support.

Much of "Long Black Song" centers upon actions involving Silas directly. However, Wright often shifts attention to Sarah, employing a stream-of-consciousness technique for her part in the preseduction and seduction scenes with the salesman. In a conversation with the salesman before the actual seduction, Sarah at one point answers the salesman's query about how she is able to keep time without a clock by replying, "We git erlong widout time."[22] Her statement contains a stubborn hope of the Negro that Wright implies had not changed since, perhaps, the American slavery days. It is a concept echoed later by Wright in his text accompanying his pictorial-textual history of the Negro, *12 Million Black Voices* (1941). There he calls Negro life an island in a sea of white faces, and he writes, "As three hundred years of time has borne our nation into the twentieth century, its rocky boundaries have remained unyielding to the waves of hope that dash against it."[23] But Sarah yields, and Silas returns to act out his revenge. His decision to stand up and fight the white man is in contrast to Sarah's submission to the salesman. Whereas Wright, through Silas, infuses a certain grandeur of Negro character into the story, Silas's death undercuts the picture; and, ironically, the weaker Negro—Sarah—is allowed to live, whether or not ridden by guilt we never know. Meanwhile, Wright maintains the vision of a domineering and cruel white world, although the justification for Silas's murder of the salesman is hardly convincing.

At the end of the short story "Down by the Riverside," Mann, like Silas, is killed after having shot to death a white man. However, Wright has created in Mann a central character whose violent revenge upon the white man is mitigated by his humane solutions to the various dilemmas he must face. Although Mann has killed, he has done so in order to save others. The story is set in a flood-besieged Southern rural town, and it lends itself to the innuendoes of a flood parable. Certainly the name "Mann" may suggest a heroic prototype figure; and the presence of a pregnant woman, Mann's wife Lulu, who will never be delivered of her child, adds dimension to the parabolic elements. Unfortunately, "Down by the Riverside" is beset too much by coincidence to make the parable artistically successful, although the swift movement and intensity of the plot matches the raging flood waters that sweep around the characters. Nevertheless, Mann remains memorable, evoking both sympathy and empathy from the reader.

The first dilemma Mann must face is whether to use a boat stolen from a white man by a Negro friend in order to reach the medical attention Lulu so desperately needs. Mann decides to risk his life for Lulu and the unborn child. With almost superhuman strength he battles the currents of the seething river, only to be confronted by Heartfield, the very white man whose boat has been stolen. The white man does not, cannot in fact, comprehend that Negro lives are worth preserving; and he heartlessly claims the boat at gun point. When Mann shoots Heartfield, he knows that he himself is as good as dead, but the forfeiture of his own life has been a sacrifice for others. Later in the night, his misdeed not yet detected by the whites and his wife now dead without giving birth, Mann must decide whether or not to rescue from an imperiled house the wife and two children of the man he has killed—the three people who recognize him as Heartfield's murderer. Again he decides to save others, although he almost turns upon his would-be accusers with an axe he holds in his hand. Mann, of course, is shown no mercy by those he has rescued. He is to be executed immediately through an edict issued by the white men in command under martial law.

In a desperate attempt at escape, Mann is felled at the water's edge by bullets, "one black palm sprawled limply outward and upward, trailing in the brown current. . . ."[24] An insensitive and brutal white world has conspired both consciously and unconsciously to destroy Wright's Negro protagonist-hero; and more successfully than in other stories under consideration in this section, Wright has created in "Down by the Riverside" a poor, ignorant Negro who murders but who is easily forgiven by the reading audience. Concepts of justice are not confused with points of law.

Wright's condemnation of the white world was tempered by his embracement of Marxism in the 1930s. Marxism, after all, is intended for all men regardless of their color. Also, it forms its distinctions in socio-economic class, not in race. "Fire and Cloud" and "Bright and Morning Star" are Wright's most overtly Marxist-influenced stories and will be treated again in the next chapter. Here, what is important to note is that these two stories not only retain a Southern setting, but also include white characters who are not hostile to the Negro. However, Wright's portrayal of these whites is weak. They are merely cardboard figures, just as unreal and invisible as the white people in *Black Boy*. In "Fire and Cloud" the beating and whipping suffered by a Negro preacher at the hands of a vigilante white gang is vividly and bitterly exposed. No doubt intended to offset this gruesome scene is the inclusion of a white Communist organizer who sympathizes with the Negroes for the economic injustices perpetrated against them, especially during such depression-ridden times; but the Marxist's appearance is only a brief one, and he never acquires the proportions of a real person. Concluding the story is a racially integrated march on city hall led by the preacher. Precisely how the two races have arrived at cooperation in this bold venture is never explained. The Marxists have played a role, certainly, but it has been a mysterious one. So despite an artifically inserted flicker of better relations between the races through Marxist inspiration, the story is dominated by white brutality and Negro fear.

"Bright and Morning Star" powerfully conveys the pain of Negro suffering and the degradation of the Negro ego, and its intensity resulting from Wright's narrative thrust helps to compensate for a thematic split and an aesthetic flaw. A proletarian tale, it offers a favorable portrait of a white girl, Reva, who, in fact, loves the young Negro Communist Party leader, Johnny-Boy. But Reva is a thinly drawn character—just as are most of Wright's whites. However, Wright continues to picture vivid scenes of white indignities and violence performed at the expense of Negroes. The painful torture and killing of Johnny-Boy and his mother by a truculent white group is graphically described. In addition, any assuagement in Negro-white hostilities is suggested not through the white Reva or other white characters, but through Johnny-Boy's mother, who very late in the story accepts tentative hopes for social reforms through Communist Party policies and practices. Thus, despite the shadowy presence of a partisan white girl, the focus, unintentional as it may be, is upon salvation more through communism than through a reversal of white attitudes, even though an intended merging of the two forces is keynoted in a pronouncement by Johnny-Boy that is critical to the thematic direction: "Ah cant see white n Ah cant see black. . . . Ah sees rich men n Ah sees po men."[25]

Wright's short fiction of the 1930s is essentially an imaginative re-creation of the atmosphere and milieu of his childhood experiences. The fears, frustrations, and pent-up angers of the Southern Negro are posed against the sadism of the white Southerner. Until, in two of the stories, Marxism enters the lives of some of his Negroes and whites, there are no influences outside of Southern culture to alter an environment generally hostile to the black man. Each story represents a Negro reaction to the white world during a moment of crisis and, usually, of violence. Furthermore, the stories collected in *Uncle Tom's Children* are so arranged that each marks a progressive increase in resistance to their lot on the part of Negro characters or groups. "Uncle Tom's children" look less and less like "Uncle Tom." In many respects, the stories could be classified as biased sociological studies, with Negroes created as the human beings and whites as the generalized evil figures. The tone of the stories reflects Wright's attitude of protest, prefiguring his outlook in his celebrated novel of protest set in a Northern metropolis, *Native Son*.

The stories, too, are filled with the kind of literary naturalism so often linked by commentators to *Native Son*. Deterministic and materialistic forces are shown as components in an environment of external forces obstructing human freedom. Also stressed are genetic and subconscious limitations on human rationality. In *Black Boy,* Wright claims that during his brief residence in Memphis his initial perusals of serious literature were of novels by Dreiser and Sinclair Lewis. Reflecting upon the events of his youth in the South, he notes that "all my life had shaped me for the realism, the naturalism of the modern novel."[26] In his terse, dialogue-filled novellas of protestation set in what is basically the rural South, Wright seems to have combined his knowledge of the fictional forms he had met in his reading and his personal impressions of a ghastly South that was antagonistic toward the Negro. In his later writings his adoption of literary naturalism is as consistent, and a posture of protest continues to inform the narratives. Thus, Wright's short fiction of the 1930s provides a valuable introduction to the themes and techniques of his later works.

Wright left the South and went to Chicago in 1927. Ten years later he journeyed to New York, where he lived until 1945. Commenting generally about Negro life in Northern urban areas, he wrote in 1941:

It seems as though we are now living inside of a machine; days and events move with a hard reasoning of their own. We live amid swarms of people, yet there is a vast distance between people . . . that words cannot bridge. No longer do our lives depend upon the soil, the sun, the rain or the wind. . . . In the South life was different; men spoke to you, cursed you, yelled at you, or killed you. The world moved by signs we knew. But here in the North cold forces hit you and push you.[27]

A defining characteristic of the urban environment, according to Wright, was that "we go home to our Black Belts and live, within the orbit of the surviving remnants of the culture of the South, our naïve, casual, verbal, fluid folk life."[28]

In *Lawd Today*, Wright traces in minute detail a day in the life of a young married Negro male in the Black Belt of Chicago. In certain spots the novel is also a fictional rendering of Wright's personal experiences in, and reactions to, Northern city life revealed elsewhere in various autobiographical sketches about his early days in Chicago.[29] Wright does not generalize from the nightmarish incidents in the day of the novel's main figure, Jake Jackson. He does, however, set before the reader the commonplaces of existence in the Black Belt. For Wright, *Lawd Today* was really a stepping stone to his much larger artistic achievement in *Native Son*.

As a work of art, *Lawd Today* is beset by numerous shortcomings. The amount of sheer dialogue is overburdening; the meager, often-monosyllabic vocabulary is shallow and poorly descriptive; and the unrelenting stress upon the smallest of details, even to the extent of picturing the card distributions in bridge games, is tedious. The fact that Wright did not offer the novel to the public—his wife had it published after his death—may be an indication of how Wright himself felt about the quality of the work. Nevertheless, *Lawd Today* is an interesting prelude to *Native Son.* Because of it, we can imagine Wright's groping to translate his Chicago experiences into an artistic genre. The novel has two significant features: one is Wright's placing of a single Negro character at the center, while at the same time examining all of the events and objects in his environment immediately touching upon his life; the other is an absence of specific white characters who could represent threats to the central figure's being. Wright's emphasis is upon Negro people and Negro life amid the cold forces of Northern urban surroundings.

Wright does not fancy his Negroes in *Lawd Today* to be lovable creatures maintaining a philosophical cheerfulness in a land of plenty turned barren because of the Great Depression. Their happy moments arrive as relief from both the hardships and the drabness of the Black Belt; however, all too often these moments come in the forms of liquor, narcotics, and illicit sexual indulgence. The picture is so sordid that one well-known Negro literary critic was sufficiently provoked to comment that *Lawd Today* contains an overabundance of offensive stereotypes of Negro characters and life.[30] Just as the actions of Bigger Thomas in *Native Son* are socially repugnant and despicable, so are those of Jake Jackson and other Negroes in *Lawd Today*. Wright implies in both novels that framing the superstructure of society dominated by the white world is capitalism, which is a force that smothers and denudes the individual personality. *Lawd Today* is thus an attempt by Wright to draft in an artistic mode and a literary genre those messages which are all too clearly spelled out later in *Native Son*.

Jake Jackson and his friends Al, Bob, and Slim are not admirable figures. Hardly worthy of a hero's role is a central character who has tricked his wife into an abortion and then resents and beats her because of the medical expenses incurred from a resultant internal infection. Neither is a married man who borrows money early in the day only to spend it at night on a prostitute from a Negro dance hall. Wright is not creating people to be emulated or pitied. They are to be seen and understood. *Lawd Today* is not a psychological novel. It does not penetrate sympathetically into the subconscious mind. Rather, it presents Jake Jackson and his companions living in their external world. Wright identifies with his characters only insofar as they too have been influenced and affected by larger external social forces, and he does not condemn or condone the choices made by Jake. Although his short stories reveal that there are some understandable, even personally valid, courses of action for Negroes, or for white men, as a matter of fact, in *Lawd Today* the range of options is limited not only because of skin color but also because of the capitalistic social structure, the ramifications of which are most evident in an urban setting.

That Wright portrays Negroes who are not admirable means neither that he is treating Negroes in general unfavorably nor that the Jake Jacksons are the sole and inevitable personality-types functioning in a Black Belt. It does suggest, however, that Wright is directing his attentions in naturalistic fashion to a common reality of everyday life in an urban ghetto produced by much more than white attitudes toward Negroes. In a later essay Wright indicates that he had formed a new consciousness about Negro life in America after having experienced a few years of urban Chicago life. The newer and larger vision extended beyond such external events as lynchings, "Jim Crowism," and brutality. It involved "crossed-up feelings" and emotional tensions. He sensed that American Negro life was "a sprawling land of unconscious suffering, and there were but few Negroes who knew the meaning of their lives, who could tell their story."[31] Although *Lawd Today* obviously cannot tell the full meaning of Negro-ness in Chicago, it can and does depict a sufficient amount of emotional tension and unconscious suffering to accent its point about the stunted, inturned culture of the urban Negro.

The black world of *Lawd Today* is lurid and disreputable. On its periphery is the white man's land, entered by Jake and his friends only when they travel to their jobs in Chicago's central post office. After work they retreat into the noise, crime, and household tensions of the strip set aside for them by the whites. The slice of the white world that they do see combines the inherent impersonal tendencies of the city with the reality of the whites' rejection of the Negro. Thus, in the North also, Wright feels, a curtain divides the two races, a curtain that prevents all but necessary and unavoidable contacts. The barrier is not so hard and fast in the North, for black and white men work side by side in the same post-office jobs; but the Negro of the North, as Wright depicts him here, continues to be abused in one way or another. For example, one of Jake's friends asserts, "The only difference between the North and the South is, them guys down there'll kill you, and those up here'll let you starve to death."[32] Even in their government jobs the men feel they can advance only so far. As Jake watches the young white college boys working around him in the post office, he senses keenly the real barriers: "Them white boys always in a hurry to get somewhere. And soon's they get out of school they's going to be big shots. But a nigger just stays a nigger."[33] In a violent image, reminiscent of the tone and the attitude of abhorrence and outrage in Wright's short stories and in *Black Boy*, Jake ventures that

"Uncle Sam's sister was raped by a nigger," because Jake "can't figger out no other reason why the white folks hate us so."[34]

The awareness of a color curtain is strong and is reflected in private conversations among the Negro men. Combined with the prospect of never being anything but mail sorters in their jobs, it leads to frustrations that turn inward to the Black Belt. We are told that when Jake looks at the post-office building before beginning his shift at work, "deep down in him was a dumb yearning for something else; somewhere or other was something or other for him. But where? How?"[35] The ground swell of a half-conscious and desperate emotion within him can find no outlets in the white world. Jake's heated outburst against the tactics of a white inspector who discovers that Jake has incorrectly sorted some of the mail is indicative of the explosion point near which the Negroes' tempers hover, but such a display of pent-up emotion on the part of Jake serves only to provide an excuse for the white man's deciding his future in the post office during the employment uncertainties of the Great Depression. The Negroes' feelings of frustration, the anxieties over their dead-end work, the knowledge that they are "niggers" in a white society that shuts them out— all produce in the men an outer pose encouraged, expected, and accepted by the whites. It is one perceptively comprehended by one of the Negroes: "We just as well take it easy and have some fun, 'cause the white folks got us hog-tied."[36]

In his short fiction of the 1930s, Wright rarely conducts the reader through a black society existing by itself. He prefers to concentrate on those moments when the black and white worlds interact with, or react to, each other. However, in *Lawd Today*, after accounting for those hours in Jake's day when he must function away from the Black Belt, Wright explores the conditions encountered and sustained in the Belt by Jake and his companions when they seek relief from their frustrations. The final section of *Lawd Today*, the "Rats' Alley" section, is a portrait of the sensuous, the risqué, and the cheap. With cigar in mouth and liquor in hand, the young men enter the smoke-filled, jazz-pierced, marijuana-offering Negro dance hall and eatery, where pimps, prostitutes, and underworld hoodlums abound. The scene is created by Wright within a surrealistic, alcohol-influenced view of Jake. The pervasive bedlam of the atmosphere is occasionally punctuated by the shrieks, whistles, and handclaps supporting the wild and exotic dances performed by Negroes "letting loose"—a spectacle that Wright perhaps has in mind when elsewhere he comments, "Our blues, jazz, swing and boogie-woogie are our 'spirituals' of the city pavements, our longing for freedom and opportunity, an expression of our bewilderment and despair in a world whose meaning eludes us."[37] In the end, the men find themselves robbed and left brutally beaten in an alley behind the hall. Jake, his week's pay and a loan spent or stolen, returns home to his wife to provoke an argument resulting in violence and physical injury. In one day Jake has traveled full circle from the tensions of his apartment, to the rejections and frustrations met in the white world, to the ephemeral thrills and emotional releases in a Black Belt sanctuary, to the now greater distresses of his marriage.

The single dominant image running through *Lawd Today* is in the form of a historic call to freedom, which ironically falls unheeded upon Negro ears deafened by the clichés of their own speeches and the spasmodic noises of their music. Because the action occurs on Lincoln's birthday, a February day symbolically blanketed with white snow, throughout the novel radios blare loudly not only excerpts from Lincoln's addresses but lectures and commentaries delivered by professors and broadcasters. While scenes of the Civil War are reenacted verbally across sixty years of time, the Chicago Negro, released and liberated to the Northern city by the events of history, is pictured by Wright as a modern slave. He has been banished to his Black Belt to search for his humanity amid the rubble of personalities shattered under the vilification and mistreatment by a white-controlled, capitalistic, urban society.

Although *Lawd Today* is not primarily a depiction of a black world in open conflict with a white world, through the mere presence of a Black Belt, of a Jake Jackson who is jealously conscious of a different circle of existence outside of the Belt, the novel does suggest an environment related to that of the black bands of Negro life spread across the Southern countryside or concentrated in tight pockets within Southern towns. To be sure, in the Northern city a threat of instantaneous death at the hands of unpredictable whites is not present, as it is in *Black Boy* and in Wright's short stories of the 1930s. Yet, the pronounced but subtle strangulation of the Negro personality within a jungle of city industries, sidewalks, and back alleys—the message behind the grim, heavy, naturalistic ploddings of Wright in *Lawd Today*—is obviously linked to the white man and the friction of race relations. The hurdle in time and space from the depressing and dangerous domain of his short stories and of *Black Boy* led Wright to experiences and visions of the Northern milieu that caused him to cry out in protest. Although the protest is muted in *Lawd Today* by his reportorial and journalistic technique, it is implanted within the author's selection of his subject matter.

Wright's second novel, *Native Son*, made him famous. Since it was issued as a monthly selection by a national book club, it received a wide circulation among the American public. It delivered powerfully to the consciousness and conscience of white America an unforgettable picture of one hideous by-product of American culture—Bigger Thomas. Furthermore, perhaps because of its extensive and, therefore, financially successful circulation, it signalled a turning point in both the subject matter and the fortunes of many Negro fiction writers in the 1940s.[38] No longer did the Negro novelist have to feel that a white audience should be patronized with portrayals of Negroes underscoring only the sentimental aspects of Negro life or an allegedly inherent, good-natured Negro acceptance of his Negro-ness and his low station in American society. Although *Native Son* was certainly not the first example of Negro protest writing in the history of American letters, its popularity and the publicity it gained undoubtedly gave encouragement and impetus to those Negro writers who would soon join the "Wright School of Protest."[39] Of course, the times were historically ripe for a *Native Son* to be received with much ado on the American literary and social scenes. The Great Depression and so much that was generated because of it—in literature, for instance, the social novels of Dos Passos, Farrell, and Steinbeck—were compelling Americans toward less romantic and more pragmatic inquiries into man's social existence and into the realities of American life. A dominant theme in literary expression was that of protest. Far from reversing a trend, *Native Son* strengthened it and advanced its demarcations into the area of race relations.

Wright's active contact with Marxism and the Communist Party had provided him with a new framework for his ideas; and his own sensitivity to, and involuntary engagement in, the plight of the Negro had afforded him with enough raw material for his fiction. Artistically, the groundwork for *Native Son* had already been established in *Lawd Today*, Wright's short fiction, and his many Marxist-oriented poems of the 1930s. Personally, a posture of protest had been adopted long before his flight into the

North, as page after page of *Black Boy* attests. Whether or not the protest novel is presently outdated as a vehicle for Negro expression is a question that James Baldwin, LeRoi Jones, and their supporters can decide only through their own art and integrity. However, still valid is Baldwin's assertion that *Native Son* is "the most powerful and celebrated statement we have yet had of what it means to be a Negro in America. . . . Such a book . . . could never have been written before. . . . Nor could it be written today. It bears already the aspect of a landmark."[40]

The plot and superficial structure of *Native Son* are respectively chronological and uncomplex. The three parts, "Fear," "Flight," and "Fate," trace: (1) the social and psychic conditions building up to Bigger Thomas's involvement in the death of a white girl, Mary Dalton; (2) Bigger's flight from the police with a Negro girl, his murder of this Bessie Mears, and his capture by the police; and (3) his trial, which allows his Marxist lawyer, Boris Max, to bombard Bigger and society with political propaganda. Beyond the plot and the violence of the novel and the polemics of the final section, what *Native Son* is in a larger sense has been subject to a diversity of opinion. Some early reviewers went so far as to assert that the novel represented a malicious tract devoted to encouraging and increasing the black man's hatred of whites.[41] To clarify what he thought were incorrect interpretations of *Native Son* and of his own intentions, Wright responded publicly with articles and letters. He emphatically affirmed that he was not defending Bigger's actions. He instead was trying to explain them through depiction. The general nature of the novel, he claimed, is a tale of a Negro youth who hated and feared whites. Bigger's hatred is to be understood as an outgrowth of his fear.[42] Beyond the broader implications of *Native Son* then, underlying the novel is a fear-hate combination earlier posed by Wright in the Southern settings of his short stories and insinuated in *Lawd Today*. Writing as late as the 1950s, James Baldwin, Wright's ofttimes detractor, validated as real for Negroes the emotion of hatred placed at the center of the novel:

There is . . . no Negro living in America who has not felt, briefly or for long periods, with anguish sharp or dull, . . . simple, naked and unanswerable hatred; who has not wanted to smash any white face he may encounter in a day, to violate, out of motives of the cruelest vengeance, their women, to break the bodies of all white people and bring them low, as low as that dust into which he himself has been and is being trampled.[43]

Although a potential Marxist salvation is inserted too obtrusively into the final section of *Native Son*—to the detriment of the artistic worth of the novel—the basic reality of the fear-hate background of race relations in America never fades.

Reshaping an element of the "Rats' Alley" section concluding *Lawd Today*, Wright opens *Native Son* with the grotesque scene of Bigger's chasing and killing the rat prowling his family's one-room, slum apartment in Chicago's Black Belt. The action is ironically symbolic. Later Bigger will assume the role of a hunted animal, and the rat will be interchanged in the minds of the whites with Negroes in general. Quickly Wright sets Bigger apart from the sharing of any warm and strong associations with members of his own family and of his young gang companions. When Bigger dangles the rat in front of his sister, Vera, to scare her, he adds to a list of annoyances that have already alienated her; and his mother's outward relationship with him is epitomized by her declaration, "Bigger, honest, you the most no-countest man I ever seen in my life."[44] His gang companions feel that he is different, that his hot temper raises a block between an open relationship between them and him. Throughout the novel, Wright focuses his attention upon Bigger and how he encounters the white world and is met by it. Baldwin has offered an appropriate comment that Wright had cut away an important dimension of Negro life, "the relationship Negroes bear to one another, that depth of involvement and unspoken recognition of shared experience which creates a way of life."[45] Baldwin's statement, however, does not weaken the premises and purposes of the novel.

Although Bigger is estranged from both the religion and the folk culture of his race, and Wright clearly and quickly establishes this fact in the novel, Bigger can still represent the Negro in abstract in terms of Negro responses to their being placed outside of many aspects of the American Dream. In the essay *How "Bigger" Was Born*, Wright explains that Bigger is attempting "to react to and answer the call of the dominant civilization whose glitter came to him through the newspapers, magazines, radios, movies, and the more imposing sight and sound of daily American life."[46] As a Negro, Bigger is barred, Wright is plainly saying, from entering the dominant white civilization. An early scene in which the gang members look up wistfully at an airplane, wishing they too could have an opportunity to pilot it, is a symbolic rendering of the curtain between the two worlds. Though the boys realize, as Gus says, that "them white boys sure can fly," they also must hopelessly agree with Bigger's brooding comment, "Yeah. . . . They get a chance to do everything."[47] An impassioned outburst by Bigger illustrates clearly that the color curtain in *Black Boy* and the short stories has been extended by Wright to the Northern city: "Goddammit, look! We live here and they live there. We black and they white. They got things and we ain't. They do things and we can't. It's just like living in jail."[48] Such morbid observations, a result of the shared experiences of the Negroes, are soon stripped away in *Native Son*, however; for Wright sets Bigger outside of these experiences by creating him as a primitive force operating between the black and white worlds, yet existing in the first because he is a Negro.

Wright lays bare what he feels is the truth of Negro life in terms of the larger society, not what it is in itself. Ironically, Negro life is what it is because it has been forceably delegated a special position by that larger society. Bigger, then, is the "nigger," the Negro symbol, as Baldwin phrases it, in "that fantasy Americans hold in their minds when they speak of the Negro: that fantastic and fearful image which we have lived with since the first slave fell beneath the lash."[49] If Bigger, as Wright has created him, is a metaphor, if he is a symbolic monster who as either a person or a fictional character cannot accept his own humanity, as Baldwin contends, then the success of *Native Son* must depend on these premises, not upon whether the protest novel is the correct medium for contemporary Negro writers or whether the protest novel lacks the reality of a believable and developing personality at its center. Furthermore, as we shall see in a later chapter, Bigger may be taken on his own terms, especially if one is willing to equate elements of modern existential philosophy with elements of Bigger's beliefs. Bigger, in fact, is a prefiguration of the existential hero Cross Damon in Wright's *The Outsider* (1953). Although Bigger is stationed outside of the Negro folk culture, he carries within him the fears, hatreds, and frustrations of his black culture. His position is not unlike that of Wright at the end of *Black Boy*, where he has rejected much of Negro life, including the quiet acceptance of Negro-ness on the part of members of his family. Like Wright, Bigger hovers in a no-man's-land between white and black, but he is imbued through experience and observation with the humilities and the suppressed reaction to them that appear to reside in every Negro breast.

At the beginning of *Native Son*, Bigger realizes that because he is a Negro the span of his life can spell out only nonfulfillment. Behind this knowledge lurks an impulse to break violently through the barriers imposed upon a whole life: "He knew that the moment he allowed what his life meant to enter fully into his consciousness, he would either kill himself or someone else."[50] A corollary is his deep desire "to merge himself with others and be part of this world, to lose himself in it so he could find himself, to be allowed a chance to live like others, even though he was black."[51] Thus, despite his estrangement from the warmth that possibly could emanate from within his own black culture, he does embody the two strains that Wright apparently thought are common to Negro-ness—the sense of frustration caused by the restrictions maintained and guarded by the whites and the wish, albeit buried or bludgeoned into the subconscious, to participate unnoticed within the whole group.

Bigger is far more than a mere singular individual whose story is to be enacted in melodramatic fashion. Just as the novel moves around such primitive symbols as the sun, water, wind, and fire, the main character proceeds through his experiences as a primitive representative of what Wright felt underlies Negro existence in America.[52] When Bigger and his gang plot to rob a white-owned and -operated store, he is overcome by the fear of reprisal from an alien white world, and he foils the attempt. When later he is invited by the white Mary Dalton and her Marxist boyfriend, Jan Erlone, to communicate with them on a personal and private level, he chokes up with a fear and a shame that accompany his awareness that he is a Negro. It is when Bigger is set loose, when he acquires an inner power to destroy both white and black life, when he is presented the occasion to plot alone against the white world, that Wright combines Bigger's search for a meaningful identity with the specter of a violent rebellion of Negro America against white America. The "act of creation" that Bigger sees in his quasi-accidental killing of Mary *is* creative. It raises him, and with him his Negro-ness, from the level of obscurity to the realm of recognition. He accomplishes alone something sensational. In so doing, he projects his now unavoidable presence into the white world. His satisfaction is, of course, perverse; but, Wright implies, it is legitimate —the logical outcome of an acknowledged release from a consciously subservient group. "Normal" morality and law are suspended for Bigger, as Wright—through such means as the lawyer Max—forges the impression that a higher law justifies Bigger's deeds. Even the "immorality" of Bigger's subsequent murder of the Negro girl, Bessie, is complicated by the reader's feeling that Bigger has, for his own good, been set free from his former fear and guilt obsessions. He is now embued with a manliness and pride of a new self. The two murders are "the most meaningful things that had ever happened to him. . . . Never had he had the chance to live out the consequences of his actions; never had his will been so free as in this night and day of fear and murder and flight."[53]

With the release of the new Bigger, the "new nigger" really, Wright betokens for white America the horrendous vision of the potential black uprising that he thought awaits in every Negro heart to be sparked against the centuries of white injustices and maltreatments. The decision to stand up and fight made by Silas in the Southern setting of "Long Black Song" Wright extends into the snowy, white, winter, urban setting of *Native Son*, with its shadowy background of the Black Belt earlier portrayed in *Lawd Today*. He suggests what could happen if the young Jake Jacksons and Bigger Thomases should choose to push their fears, frustrations, and hatreds outward into the whole society rather than inward into the Black Belt. Thus Bigger's tale, metaphorically affecting as it does an entire nation, is epic, its actions symbolizing decisions on the grand scale.[54]

Employing the omniscient narrative device within the naturalistic framework of *Native Son*, Wright transplants in one way or another most of the aspects of American race relations previously outlined in his short stories and *Lawd Today*. For example, the connections made by Southern whites between Negro manliness and the defense of white maidenhood are duplicated in the Northern urban environment. Newspaper headlines publicize the possible rape of Mary by Bigger; and, at the trial, as long-winded as it is because of the employment of the lawyer Max as a Marxist spokesman and interpreter of Bigger's life, the state's attorney, Buckley, proclaims that "the central crime here is *rape!* Every action points toward that!"[55] Bigger is able to conceal his part in Mary's disappearance from the Dalton household by hiding behind another fiction about Negro life maintained by the whites: that a Negro would not dare, in fact would not be smart enough, to kill a rich white girl. Wright himself later elaborates on the implications of such a distorted view:

The entire long scene in the furnace room is but a depiction of how warped the whites have become through oppression of Negroes. If there had been *one* person in the Dalton household who viewed Bigger Thomas as a human being, the crime would have been solved in half an hour. Did not Bigger himself know that it was the denial of his personality that enabled him to escape detection so long?[56]

Furthermore, Bigger helps to preserve the white fiction by acting out as long as he can the white-assigned role of the harmless, stupid black boy. He feels that "who on earth would think that he, a black timid Negro boy, would murder and burn a rich white girl and would sit and wait for his breakfast like this?"[57] This guise is a variation of the similar one that Wright in *Black Boy* found he had to assume to survive in the Southern culture.

Native Son differs, however, from the autobiography and from most of the earlier writings in an important respect: a conscious attempt is made by Wright to picture certain whites as human beings sympathetic to and communicating with Negroes. In the first part of the novel, encountered again is a Negro vision of whites similar to that in Wright's short fiction and *Black Boy*, that "to Bigger and his kind white people were not really people; they were a sort of natural force, like a stormy sky looming overhead."[58] Near the end of the novel we see that in Jan Erlone, Bigger has discovered that "for the first time in his life a white man became a human being to him."[59] Then we are also asked to believe that Boris Max has exuded such a genuine warmth and interest that he too is transformed in Bigger's mind from a symbol of the threatening natural force into a human being. Unfortunately, not only does Wright draw a paper-thin characterization of Jan throughout the novel, he so overdramatically utilizes Max as an orator of Marxist doctrine that he thoroughly undermines Max's effectiveness as a living character.

Max's courtroom plea for Bigger's life is not solely Marxist propaganda. Max often seems caught between a purely economic interpretation of Negro-white relations and an interpretation taking into account noneconomic, psychological, and irrational factors. Reiterating many points Wright has introduced elsewhere in the novel, Max mentions the social, educational, and economic restrictions placed upon Negroes by the whites. He also contends that Negroes "constitute a separate nation, stunted, stripped, and held captive *within* this nation, devoid of political, social, economic, and property rights."[60] Max thinks that most Negroes, like Bigger, want to attain self-realization

and dignity; however, because of the whites' firm and cruel
domination over them, they can feel only fear and hatred.
In many respects, then, he is reasoning that Bigger's crimes
have been predetermined. They are logical responses to
the harsh barriers constructed by whites between Negroes
and the rest of the society.

It is when Max deals with the history of American
Negro-white relations that he resorts to Marxist explanations. However, he does recognize that the whites too are
possessed by a fear of Negroes and by strong guilt feelings
over the history of their rule over blacks. Although fear
and guilt are rational motives for white actions, they have
caused irrational deeds to be heaped upon the original misdeed of forcing the Negro to exist outside the whole society.
Thus, Max is trying to cope with interpretations that seem
to start from a Marxist historical view but are often sustained by noneconomic factors—much in the manner that
Wright later treats his nonfictional folk history of the
American Negro in *12 Million Black Voices* (as we shall
discover in Chapter 2). However, Max reveals, the culprit
behind all is capitalism. It has produced "men of wealth,"
who urge a show of white force and intimidation in order
"to protect a little spot of private security against the resentful millions from whom they have filched it." Capitalism and the property class have conspired in a diversionary
action to foster white involvement in the suppression of the
Negro so that the whites themselves might feel that they
are protecting the American Dream, the dream that Max
thinks is actually part of a plot against all men without
property, whites and blacks.[61] He suggests that the answer
to problems even more fundamental than race relations lies
in a Marxist revolution.

Despite an apparent alteration in Wright's outlook on
the future of race relations, the world of *Native Son* is essentially like that of his earlier works, a world divided by

a color curtain. A Bigger Thomas released from the social restraints imposed upon his color is the significant difference. If Wright complained that he had previously written with *Uncle Tom's Children* "a book which even bankers' daughters could read and weep over and feel good about," then with *Native Son* he satisfied his oath to write a novel that "no one would weep over," that "would be so hard and deep that they would have to face it without the consolation of tears."[62]

During the twenty years between *Native Son* and Wright's death, he spent more time and effort on nonfiction than on fiction. Only one of his three novels in this period, *The Long Dream*, extensively treats American race relations; and the best single piece among his few short stories and radio scripts, "The Man Who Lived Underground," tells us less about Negro-white relations than about Wright's metaphysics. *Eight Men*, a posthumously issued collection, contains all the stories and scripts of Wright's last two decades, plus a couple of his earlier stories. They cover a span of about twenty-five years and are set in both the American South and North and in such foreign locations as Africa, Paris, and Copenhagen. Addressed primarily to white Americans, they are best characterized by Wright's declaration in 1945 that unless white Americans change their ways, they will soon be facing overt Negro violence against them.[63]

The violence of the stories in *Eight Men* has been criticized by James Baldwin. Not only does he feel that it is gratuitous and compulsive, but he also condemns Wright's failure to explore the roots of that violence, which, Baldwin claims, are the inner rages of the author and of the fictional characters. He does congratulate Wright for uncovering the sexual myths proliferated around the American Negro, suggesting that when Wright pays great heed to the details of physical destruction, he is stressing the Negro's "terrible attempt to break out of the cage which the American imagination has imprisoned him for so long."[64]

The details in "The Man Who Was Almost a Man," a short story included in *Eight Men*, relate to the rural culture of the Southern Negro.[65] They are vaguely reminiscent of the flight elements in *Black Boy*. The seventeen-year-old David wants to be treated as an adult by other Negroes in the rural community; and by owning a gun against his parents' wishes, he possesses a symbol of maturity and of rebellion against parental authority. After he has accidentally shot a mule owned by his white employer and has been chastised by his parents, he must live with the haunting memories of a white crowd that has laughed at him because of his foolish actions. Finding the strain too pressing, he steals off into the night and boards a passing freight train, presumably northward bound. The tale suggests that the whites are the overlords who force the Negro personality inward toward its own separate culture group. Although the Negro parents who do not understand the needs of their son could, of course, be any parents, white or black, there is the slightest suggestion that these Negro parents feel the white burden above them and are thus unable to communicate openly with their own kin. The heckling and laughing white crowd is only a stage prop used by Wright to symbolize the amusement afforded the whites by confused Negroes. The result is not unification and communication among Southern blacks; rather, it is the flight from the South—from the environment that has produced their frightened and fragmented black culture—a re-echoing of the final pages of *Black Boy*.

"The Man Who Killed a Shadow" deals with the real and shadow lives of Saul Saunders, a Negro born in a small Southern town who subsequently becomes aware of "a world . . . split in two, a white world and a black one, the white one being separated from the black by a million psychological miles."[66] Later, as a middle-aged janitor in Washington's National Cathedral, he is continually distracted by the sexually suggestive antics of a forty-year-old, virgin, white librarian. One day, after being called "black nigger" by her, he experiences a swift resurgence of the submerged responses to a lifetime of buried humilities. In a surrealistic scene, he brutally kills the librarian and mutilates her body. Although the blond, blue-eyed Miss Houseman, like the laughing white crowd in "The Man Who Was Almost a Man," is an undeveloped, symbolic stage prop, the outburst of animalistic violence directed against her by Saul Saunders is a figurative representation of another possible Negro reaction to generations of white suppression and of white sexual myth perversion. Like Bigger Thomas and many of Wright's Negro characters, Saul has looked "timidly out from his black world" to see "the shadowy outlines of a white world that was unreal to him and not his own."[67] The single moment of uncontrollable rage bursts out into the white world in the form of hideous violence, as Saul, symbolically all Negroes, destroys the shadow that has covered him all his life. The story is a warning to whites, a timeworn tale told elsewhere and often by Wright in one shape or another. Its publication date, 1949, bares a consistent attitude toward American Negro-white relations on the part of the author.

Baldwin feels that "Man of All Work"—the last short fictional work written by Wright—is a masterpiece and a sign that Wright, "as he died, was acquiring a new tone, and a less uncertain esthetic distance, and a new depth."[68] Wright's portrayal of a Negro man who, unable to find a job and relying on the income from his wife's work, dresses in his wife's clothes and hires himself out as a cook, penetrates deeply into the demoralization of the Negro male and the fragmentation occurring within a family when the female plays the role of the breadwinner.[69] To a certain extent the interior of Negro culture is being examined in this radio-play script.[70] However, the plot stresses the events that materialize when the Negro Carl enters the home and the daily routine of the white Fairchild family. Mr. Fairchild's imagined stereotype of promiscuous Negro women and his belief that a Negro woman will want to submit to his advances because he is white and thus powerful lead to a humorous situation, recalling British Restoration drama: a man chasing another man who is disguised as a woman. In due time a jealous Mrs. Fairchild arrives on the scene and helps to disentangle the confused state of affairs by wounding Carl with a bullet. Medical assistance is rendered to the injured Negro, and he returns home, a wiser man for his troubles. Other than the two-hundred-dollar check he receives to save the Fairchild family from public scandal, Carl gains nothing more than a reinforcement of his knowledge that the white world is a perilous habitat for Negroes, and that white men would affront the dignity of black women by assuming that they all are promiscuous. Wright maintains the vision of a hostile and ignorant white world; however, the significant aspect of "Man of All Work" is not in the treatment of themes but in the added dimension of the humor of situation. In this radio script, which lacks authorial intrusions, we see hints of a change in Wright's artistic approach, which death never permitted him to develop. Baldwin's remarks are both pertinent and incisive in this respect.

Wright's novel *The Long Dream* lacks the narrative force of *Native Son*. Although it too was written in a vein of protest, it appeared during a decade in which other Negro novelists were beginning to deal with a wider scope of the American-Negro experience. Accordingly, *The Long*

Dream suffered from criticisms that often overlooked some of the accomplishments of the novel. Reviewer Granville Hicks has pointed out the undue melodrama, the unpolished prose style, and the weak characterization of Fishbelly Tucker, the central figure, who seems to mature too quickly.[71] Saunders Redding feels, and justifiably so, that the novel has a major weakness of iteration, that Wright insists the reader be told repeatedly the implications of the plot.[72] Redding's severest attack on *The Long Dream* revolves around the idea that Wright in his Paris exile had lost touch with his American roots and thus could not accurately account for either subtle or dramatic changes in race relations in the States.[73] In *The Long Dream*, Wright does return to the Southern world of *Black Boy* and his early short fiction; and Fishbelly's flight to Paris at the end of the novel mirrors conclusions in other of Wright's works and also parallels his own self-exile.

Thematically, *The Long Dream* characterizes a relationship between the whites and the blacks of the South distinguished again by a curtain drawn by the ruling whites. Threats and dangers to Negro property, life, and personality are unrelentingly present. However, the novel differs from Wright's other fiction in two ways: it depicts a middle-class, entrepreneur Negro existence, and it portrays the psychological and emotional growth of a central figure over a period of time. Artistically noteworthy are the ironies in dialogue and action and the inclusion of mirrored episodes.

The action takes place in Clintonville, Mississippi, a town of twenty-five thousand inhabitants, ten thousand of whom are Negroes. Tyree Tucker, Fishbelly's father, is a prospering middle-class businessman whose facade enterprise is a funeral parlor. However, a substantial portion of his income is derived from dwellings rented to Negroes and from a Negro whorehouse. In addition, Tyree and another Negro professional man, Dr. Bruce, own a dance hall, which is another haven of entertainment and prostitution for Clintonville's Negroes. For ten years a monthly check has been given by Tyree and Dr. Bruce to Gerald Cantley, the white chief of police, to permit the illicit operations in the shabby dance hall to continue unhindered. When a Fourth-of-July fire destroys the dance hall in the 1950s, forty-two Negroes perish, triggering a chain of events that includes the murder of Tyree and the emergence of Fishbelly as the manager of the Tucker businesses.

The first two sections, about three-quarters of *The Long Dream*, are occupied with Fishbelly's relationship with his father and his impressions of what a Negro must do in order to live safely in the South. The final section deals with Fishbelly's contacts with whites and the events turning his fear and suppressed hatred and jealousy of whites into flight. His escape from Mississippi mirrors Fishbelly's earlier discovery that Southern whites "lived with niggers, shared with them, worked with them, but owed them no human recognition."[74] It also reflects his dream of entering a social realm in which his safety is ensured and his ability to accumulate money and material goods is not stifled. Fishbelly is fatally in love with the white world, because the white world could offer him the chance to develop his personality and his wealth without fear of reprisal from a racial group. The fact that he flees directly to Paris, bypassing the American North, represents a commentary by Wright on the racial climate of Northern cities and conveys an insight supported later by actual racial violence in the North.

Tyree Tucker has been able to uplift his family through smart though occasionally unethical business dealings. Although he possesses a house, cars, and property holdings equal to those of many middle-class whites of the town, he does so only by exploiting members of his own race. In addition, he must depend upon an uneasy alliance with the white powers of the town to maintain his position. Operating within a Negro proverb that the "white folks are on top of us, and our own folks are on top of our folks, and God help the black man on the bottom," he knows that he can reach merely the lower perimeter of the white world. His security is possible only because he has money to bribe many whites from destroying him and his business ventures. Meanwhile, Fishbelly in his youth, like the young Wright in *Black Boy*, slowly perceives the truth of his father's belief but inwardly rebels against the adverse implications for the full development of his own personality.

A fascinating aspect of the novel is Fishbelly's movement from this rebellion to acceptance. A disgust that had overcome him when his father was forced to act humbly and subserviently in front of the chief of police and the mayor is transformed in time into Fishbelly's willingness to act out the role of vassal to the white world. The moment of conversion occurs when Fishbelly, brought to jail for trespassing on white property and then playfully threatened with castration by white policemen, is released only after Tyree has pleaded with his white connections to drop the charges. Fishbelly then comprehends that his father all along has been doing the only thing possible for a Negro who wishes a measure of independence in the South. Earlier he had felt that his father was a symbolically castrated man. Now that he himself has been compelled to face real castration, he believes that his safety is bound up in the acquisition of money and the acceptance of his father's pragmatic philosophy that "the only way to git along with white folks is to grin in their goddamn faces and make 'em feel good and then do what the hell you want to behind their goddamn backs!"[75]

To this point in the novel, Wright has pictured both the perpetuation of white hostility and domination and the continuation of the Negro's fatalistic response to them from one generation to the next. Fishbelly's hatred and disgust for his father's acceptance of servility is changed into an admiration for the cunning and intelligence that have made that position secure. However, the irony lies in the channeling of Negro energies and frustrations into efforts of cheating other Negroes in order to please whites, thus reinforcing the structure of the segregated society. Wright successfully uses two recurrent images—parasites and castration—to illustrate the nature of the whole society and the white threats that help to keep it as it is. If Wright's earlier depiction of the South of the 1920s and 1930s was characterized by fear and buried hatred on the part of poor Negroes, that of the 1950s is featured by more of the same, but now on the part of middle-class Negroes. Corruption and exploitation now become sins shared by both whites and blacks.

Following the dance-hall fire, in which Fishbelly has lost his light-colored Negro mistress, Tyree engages Chief of Police Cantley in a game of blackmail. The cancelled checks held by Tyree are pitted against Cantley's influence with the jury that will try Tyree for the criminal negligence responsible for the fire. After Cantley has arranged for and supervised Tyree's murder, Fishbelly has the option of using his large share of the inheritance or of fleeing the town. But Fishbelly is blinded by the glitter of the possible gold he could gain by continuing both his father's corrupt arrangement with Cantley and the operation of the whorehouse, and he elects to stay in Clintonville. One generation of Negroes replaces another, and the white-dominated system remains unthreatened by revolt or unweakened by escape. Chief Cantley's next move is to discover whether Fishbelly has the cancelled checks; and Fishbelly, imitating his father in a way that previously had repulsed him, falls down on his knees before Cantley, pleading and crying that he would not betray a white man. Again Wright creates a mirror effect from one Tucker to the next, symbolizing the continuing fate of the Southern Negro.

At last Fishbelly is caught in a situation that recalls to him Tyree's shouted proclamation: *"You are nothing because you are black, and proof of your being nothing is that if you touch a white woman, you'll be killed!"*[76] Cantley prearranges to have Fishbelly found with a white woman. Fishbelly is caught and, through the working of white juries and laws, is sentenced to jail for two years. There, away from his money-making operations in Clintonville, he begins to see what exactly his Negro life in the South has been. Not even the power and authority of comparative wealth have been sufficient to secure a safe existence. Instead, he finds an earlier conviction of his youth confirmed—a conviction he had somewhere dismissed in his later selfish desires to accumulate the money he foolishly thought would buy him life and dignity. He now understands that the white world "had the power to say who could or could not live and on what terms; and the world in which he and his family lived was a kind of shadow world."[77] Like Wright at the end of *Black Boy*, Fishbelly flees the hostile South, "yearning to be at last somewhere at home," yearning to find a place that would allow his personality to develop within a whole society, not a fragmented and racially segregated one.[78]

The Long Dream is a protest novel. As such, it makes little distinction between the Negro-white relations Wright grew to comprehend during the days of his youth described in *Black Boy* and the relations he could only read about and sense during his final years in Paris. *The Long Dream* reiterates a consistent Wright theme that in America a curtain hangs between the black and white races. This curtain is not only an outgrowth of white prejudice, but also a barrier against the elimination of that prejudice through communication between the races. Furthermore, it creates an impediment to the full development and expression of all American Negroes. Seeing injustices heaped upon the Negro and recognizing the denial of humanity to the Negro, a tortured Wright must cry out in rage—a rage, as James Baldwin pronounces, that is almost literally the howl of a man being castrated.[79] Wright's bitterness at the history and the course of relations between the two races is as noticeable and intrusive in his final novel as it is in nearly everything he had published. Despite the naturalistic techniques and the use of the third-person, omniscient narrator, an aesthetic and philosophic distance between the author and his material is never achieved—in *The Long Dream* or nearly every other piece by Wright concerned with American race relations. Even when the dialectics of Marxism, to be transformed into social action, offered Wright a hope for parting the color curtain, he reverted to the attitudes he had acquired in his youth in the South and in his early adulthood among the Black Belt inhabitants of Chicago. In the absence of the tempering influence of Marxism, a feeling of outrage thoroughly permeates *The Long Dream*.

When we listen to Wright telling us about the worlds of black and white in America, we may hear echoes from a poem that he wrote in the 1930s, "Between the World and Me." In it the persona stumbles upon the remains of a tarred-and-feathered Negro. Soon the dry bones and the gray ashes begin to sink into the persona himself, and he imagines that he too is battered by white hands. Then, after being tied to a sapling, coated with hot tar, punctured by white feathers, and drenched in gasoline, he is set afire. The poem ends with begging and pain—the cry of a man agonized by the sight of man's inhumanity to man.[80] This pain and agony, whether real or imagined, characterizes Richard Wright's treatment of American race relations. It underlies the protest of a black man who would sacrifice, perhaps unintentionally, the preciousness of his art for the birth of humane justice in his native land. However, as a cry of pain within protest writing, it seeks a justice that Wright felt was within the scope of human achievement. Other aspects of his work indicate as much.

CHAPTER 2

Marxism, the Party,
and a Negro Writer

IN THE MIDDLE of the nineteenth century Karl Marx was formulating for the working classes a program for mass social unheavals based upon the philosophical dialectics of the Hegelian triad. The American Southern Negro was then still a slave in a regional society maintaining, in Marxist terms, its feudal roots amid a burgeoning capitalism. By 1908, when Richard Wright was born, the South had lost in battle its right to sustain slavery. Furthermore, a hitherto basically agrarian Southern economy was witnessing the rapid encroachment of capitalistic techniques and pragmatic philosophy upon its once-genteel, semifeudal order.

Whether or not the Southern milieu had settled into a particular pattern outlined by Marx and his successors made no difference to the young Wright. As *Black Boy* reveals, he thought of himself as only a black American in a white world, and he began to acquire the fears, frustrations, and suppressed drives implied in that unique social structure. Poverty Wright knew. He had gone hungry more than once, wondering too "why some people had enough food and others did not."[1] However, certainly, such a concern does not automatically lead to an adoption of Marxist doctrine as a cure for social ills. Nor does the existence of poverty and a caste system within a national capitalistic economic framework offer proof in itself for the validity of the historical theories propounded by Marx and Engels. Indeed, if nothing else, Southern slavery and the succeeding caste system based on color have a history that defies the methodical categories of historical change identified through Marxism. However, Marxism is a revolutionary call directed toward oppressed peoples everywhere, and its potential appeal to American Negroes is self-evident. Nevertheless, as Wilson Record had concluded in his well-known study of American Negroes and the Communist Party, Negroes have generally chosen to protest within the constitutional framework for a variety of reasons, including their adverse reactions to Party control from Moscow and to the fluctuations in official Party attitudes toward the importance of American racial problems.[2]

Richard Wright, though, was one Negro who for more than a decade did embrace the hope, if not some of the tenets, in Marxist doctrine. His contact with Marxism did not occur in the South but in the North, after his flight to Chicago less than two years before the inception of the Great Depression. It was during the depression that Wright, working at odd jobs but fascinated by literature and the prospect of a literary career, learned about the John Reed Club of Chicago. Negro friends had informed him that the club was sponsoring a literary journal, *Left Front*, and that no distinctions were being made between black and white talent. Although Wright discovered that the club was dominated by Party members, he decided to attend a meeting but approached it with skepticism: "I felt that the Communists could not possibly have a sincere interest in Negroes. I was cynical and I would rather have heard a white man say that he hated Negroes, than to have heard him say that he respected Negroes, which would have made me doubt him."[3] However, a warm reception by club members and their apparently immediate acceptance of Wright as an equal, aspiring young artist softened his attitude. He soon became interested in Communist literary journals and then the philosophical and political traits of Marx and Engels.

Through his readings Wright perceived a connection between his experiences as a Negro in America and those of the oppressed working classes of the world: "It was not the economics of Communism," he was to write, "nor the great power of trade unions . . . that claimed me." Instead, his imagination was captured "by the similarity of the experiences of workers in other lands, by the possibility of uniting scattered but kindred peoples into a whole." Thus, he continued, "at last, in the realm of revolutionary expression, Negro experience could find a home."[4] Constance Webb, Wright's biographer and close friend, helpfully adds that during the period of Wright's Party activities—from 1934 to 1942—he came to believe in "the essence of Communism," which to him conveyed "brotherhood, universality, hope of harmony, universal reason and an assumption of natural immutable moral laws."[5] Wright's interpretation of what Marxism stood for is, in fact, a summary catalogue of those elements which later became increasingly evident as the components of his vision for an ideally functioning modern world.

Wright inserted Marxist materials and Communist Party propaganda into his publications between 1934 and 1941. By 1942 his disenchantment with the Party had become known in private circles.[6] By 1944 his anti-Party convictions were apparently so strong that he felt compelled to announce his position publicly. Wright's two-piece disavowal of the Party was printed in the *Atlantic Monthly* and later appeared in *The God That Failed* collection.

The facts of Wright's connections with the Party are not clear. Webb's biography, though it offers details not previously generally known, is, unfortunately, discursive in this respect and sets down no organized pattern of events in Wright's involvement. Further complicating matters is the time period covered in *The God That Failed* essay. That essay describes events only until Wright departed Chicago for New York in 1937. Yet, during the last half of 1937 Wright was working as a reporter for the Party organ in New York, *The Daily Worker*; and the Marxist content is pervasive in *Uncle Tom's Children* (1938), *Native Son* (1940), and *12 Million Black Voices* (1941), all published after 1937. Furthermore, Wright did state in print that "from 1932 to 1944 I was a member of the Communist Party of the United States."[7]

Wright tells us that, in part, his disagreements with the Party in Chicago did not essentially arise out of differences in belief on large issues. Rather, a conflict quickly developed over exactly how and when he should divide both his time and his creative energies between Party functions and his artistic endeavors. Wright admits concerning this period: "I wanted to be a Communist, but my kind of Communist. I wanted to shape people's feelings, awaken their hearts."[8] He found it personally more important and meaningful to use in his own way his imagination and writing skills to spread Marxism than to fulfill such time-consuming Party obligations as attending rallies and organizing committees against a high cost of living.[9]

Differences that were more radical slowly developed to replace the quarrels based seemingly on immediate practical questions. Wright describes the process in his essay in *The God That Failed*. In essence he began to object to the Party's tendency to place aims for a better society above the immediate personal needs of the individual. He did not care to be part of the generation sacrificed for the welfare of subsequent generations. Whereas he was sincerely bound up in the hopes fostered by Marx, he was also repulsed by the dubious forms assumed by actions and policies when they were derived from the philosophy, thus, of course, often deflating the philosophy itself. In the Party operation of transforming philosophy into action, Wright came to feel that something of the hope was being sacrificed. He thought that the dogmatic and mechanistic practices used by the Party in order to survive in a real world of power relationships often were undercutting the ideals of Marxism. In one respect, Wright's type of rebellion from the Party was like Trotsky's—based upon disillusionment when the Party moved from a posture of idealism to that of realism and power-consciousness.[10]

The question of the role of the artist within the Party seems to have been an initial key issue for Wright in Chicago, as we learn from his piece in *The God That Failed*. By 1944 that issue had been settled in Wright's mind. In a published letter of November 1944 to the Uruguayan painter and engraver Antonio R. Frasconi, Wright declared of the artist and his political commitments:

Must we artists have bosses, Left or Right? Cannot our art be a guide to all men of good-will who want to know the truth of our time? Cannot we artists speak in a tone of authority of our own? . . .

. . . I would warn that we must beware of those who seek, in words no matter how urgent or crisis-charged, to interpose an alien and dubious curtain of reality between our eyes and the crying claims of a world which it is our lot to see only too poignantly and too briefly.[11]

Reechoed here, in slightly varied form, is the personal conflict, artist versus Party encroachments, appearing in *The God That Failed* essay. Ten years after this public letter to Frasconi, Wright again commented on his reasons for leaving the Party, this time touching upon both deeper philosophical implications and real political affairs:

My relinquishing of membership in that Party was not dictated by outside pressure or interests; it was caused by my conviction that Marxist Communism, though it was changing the world, was changing that world in a manner that granted me even less freedom than I had possessed before. . . . When historic events disclosed that international Communism was mainly an instrument of Russian foreign policy, I . . . disassociated myself from it.[12]

One other issue that Wright raised dealt with Soviet Russia's relationship to American communism and is not elaborated here. Enough of the elements treated here, however, are found in *The God That Failed* essay to suggest that that essay is a symbolic representation of Wright's thinking between roughly the years 1941 and 1944. In any event, no one can deny that in the middle and late years of the 1930s he was so influenced by Marxism and the Communist Party that they strongly motivated his writing, especially his poetry.

Wright published sixteen poems that are most conveniently categorized as Marxist or proletarian.[13] He declared in *The God That Failed* essay that he had been intrigued with the link he perceived between his Negro experiences and those of the working classes as he understood them through his readings of Marxist materials. However, not until after he had composed his first five poems—published in such journals as *Left Front* and *The Anvil*—did he attempt to integrate poetically his Negro experiences and leftist tenets and propaganda.

Wright's earliest pieces, those of 1934, he later was to call his "crude poems."[14] Not only are they tinged with a bitter hatred for all capitalistic institutions and representatives, but they contain a multitude of violent images and actions. His later poems, though they remain propagandistic, are usually less passionate. They stress a hope and a faith in Marxism in general rather than an immediate and desperate necessity for workers' strikes and violent social upheavals. Overall, his poems move from a dogmatic Marxist militancy to a rather restrained trust in the Marxist vision.

Wright's first two poems are addressed to rich capitalists: "Rest for the Weary" speaks to "panic-stricken guardians of gold"; "A Red Love Note," to a "lovely bloated one."[15] Both prophesy an impending swift and violent revolution against capitalism. In "Strength" and in "Everywhere Burning Waters Rise," images from violent and destructive forces of nature illustrate the power and the universality of a workers' revolution by bloodshed. "Strength" moves from the image of a "gentle breeze" produced by the singular efforts of one comrade to a "raging hurricane" of united mass action against a rotten and greedy capitalism.[16] In "Everywhere Burning Waters Rise," coordinated action by angry masses of workers is prophetically expanded into an elimination of capitalistic exploitation.[17] Wright's approach in "Child of the Dead and Forgotten Gods" is an exposure of the violence perpetrated by the managers of capital through their use of club-swinging policemen. Also condemned are well-meaning but non-revolutionary liberals, who think that merely the sound of their words will be effective in combatting economic oppression.[18] Another poem, "I Have Seen Black Hands," is an interpretation of American-Negro history within the framework of the Marxist dialectic—a technique later attempted by Wright in his extended poetic prose of *12 Million Black Voices*. Revealing the exploitation of Negroes in what he feels are capitalist-sponsored wars and economic depressions, he concludes the poem by placing hope in a joint Negro-white workers' violent revolution. As in his short story "Fire and Cloud," Wright stresses in this poem cooperation between blacks and whites. He foresees the establishment of an interracial link between blacks and whites through their shared perception of an oppressive and color-blind capitalistic economic structure. The Marxist program for action, Wright implies, will cut through racial lines and will help to create, among other things, a homogeneous society on "some red day" in the future.[19]

In "Ah Feels It in Mah Bones," Wright works through the oral dialect of an uneducated Negro to suggest the existence of a potentially revolutionary consciousness, even among those Negroes ignorant of Marxist doctrine—a majority no doubt. The black narrator senses that violent change is about to occur, and he proclaims that he is ready and willing to join the revolution.[20] Here Wright shifts his poetic tactics from a contrived dependence on the formal terminology of Marxism and the loud propaganda phrases of the Party to a more subtle rendering of a Negro mass consciousness of the wrongs and injustices within a capitalistic system. The stress is on general social injustice, not on racial prejudice.

A motif of hope emerges in Wright's poetry of 1935. These poems are often surrounded by "sunshine" and "new dawns." In "Red Leaves of Red Books," Wright describes a physical process and turns it into a political metaphor. Leafing its way through pages of Marxist books, a world of men and women, young and old, educates itself for a revolutionary role by reading the "printed hope" offered it by the Marxists.[21] "Spread Your Sunrise!" also portrays a metaphorical physical event: a "giant child"— communism—comes out of Soviet Russia on a mythical journey through the nations of the world to paint them red with hope.[22]

These two poems have little to do with Negro experience

as such, and they remain propagandistic pieces. However, evident in them is a shift away from ostensible militancy. The poet's treatment of his Marxist material is again more subtle than in his first poems. Even a later poem, "We of the Streets," is handled more through a poet's voice than a politician's shout, even though it pictures at its conclusion a mass of city workers marching in the streets. It manages to project an atmosphere of sensuous sounds and sights, and Wright focuses optimistically on the promise of a Marxist society, not on bitter indictments of capitalism or on rabid fomentations of violent revolution.[23]

"Old Habit and New Love," published in 1936, is significant for two reasons: it suggests Wright's movement away from political dogma, and it indicates his own awareness that he was an artist first and a political man second. Wright employs the language of the machine age. He also replaces former visions of revolution and violent actions with the concept that the twentieth-century Marxist poet should work energetically to discover methods of transforming the unique language and images of his own time into useful implements for social change. "Hope" and "dawn"—symbols of Wright's shift to a less militant Marxist attitude—are combined with industrial-age images and words, as Wright attempts to fuse a message of the poem with his actual artistic rendering of the material.[24]

Ironically perhaps, one of Wright's finest poetic achievements is his highly propagandistic "Transcontinental."[25] It happens to be his longest poem; however, its success emanates not from length but from technique, language, and tone. Its harsh and militant pose is obvious: there are ugly name-callings and constant incitements for violent revolution. Yet the poet's strength comes from the real sense of movement in an automobile trip across the United States. A word here, a phrase there, a growing shout in front, a fading noise behind—all are captured vividly by

the poet on his journey. At intervals throughout is inter-
jected a recurrent bold shout from what could be a cheer-
leading section—"UNITEDFRONT—SSSTRIKE," and fragments of politically reactionary clichés are alternated with
Party statements or Marxist pronouncements. Although the
theme of the plight of the Negro in America is also included, it is merely one part of the main political thrust of
the poem. In content the poem is essentially propagandistic
and narrow in its intellectual approach, yet "Transcontinental" generates a feeling of excitement, speed, and mo-
tion. Significantly, it was published when Wright was
perhaps at the most feverish heights of his involvement
with the Communist Party in Chicago—less than a half
year before he was forcefully thrown out of a May Day
demonstration by more obedient members of the party.[26]

Wright's proletarian poetry, then, generally reflects a
movement from propaganda-making to poetry-making. It
tends to move from blatant Marxist and Party words to a
utilization of words for their beauty and subtle suggestive
powers. There is an obvious advance in Wright's skills and
techniques, but poetic forms apparently were not large
enough to satisfy his desire to encompass the emotion-
packed details of his Southern and Northern experiences.
They were abandoned for a concentration on the short-
story and novel forms. No doubt, too, Wright's disagreements with the Party and the continued employment in-
securities of the depression influenced him to turn to
artistic expressions more likely to reach a larger audience and thus more likely to provide him with economic
independence.

Wright's experiences in the South gave him much of the
subject matter for his early short stories, which are primarily vignettes of critical moments in black and white
relations. Stories not portraying such moments are "Super-

stition" and "Silt." Although the former is set against a background from which whites are conspicuously absent, "Silt" is a commentary on Southern racial relations. Like most of Wright's stories in the 1930s, it presents a motif associated with Marxism. The story centers on the Negro Tom, whose farm is often devastated by flood waters and who is constantly in financial debt to the white Burgess at exorbitant rates of interest, and is a reflection of more than the Negro's subservience to the domineering white man. It is also a manifestation of the cruel vise—nature at one end and capitalistic selfishness at the other—clamped upon the poor and ignorant farmer. From such rural conditions have emerged those armies of revolution which, as later disciples of Marx came to realize, could join forces with an awakened and militant urban proletariat. However, in "Silt" the spirit of revolution remains dormant. Tom, an "Uncle Tom" accepter in racial and Marxist-propagandistic terms, becomes further indebted to his usurious landlord.

In *Uncle Tom's Children*, both the first and the expanded editions, Wright generally relocates his arenas of conflict, racial and class, from the poverty-stricken farms to the small towns of the South. An exception is the setting for "Long Black Song"; however, the town is only a few hills away, and the white men whose respect Silas craves are townspeople, not farmers. This shift parallels a geographical movement in Wright's own life, which offered the live experiences from which the stories could be conceived. In addition, an urban setting provides a convenient basis for a broader Marxist application, even though, because of the geography of Wright's Southern experience, the masses of industrial workers are not incorporated into the plots. The collection of stories is most easily understood on the obvious level of racial conflict. However, as one tale leads into the next, the Marxist undertones develop progressively into functioning materials of the stories until, at last, personal fulfillment and social salvation is identified with action and hope in the Communist Party. Therefore, since the militancy of action increases with successive episodes, *Uncle Tom's Children* creates the impression of having a novel-like development.[27]

Actually, not until the third story in the original four-story collection—"Long Black Song"—do the Marxist strands begin to emerge. Earlier, in "Down by the Riverside," the National Guard troops operating through the martial law declared for the flood emergency are painted as cruel, obedient, and paid stooges of the powers who have a vested interest in maintaining the prevailing order of society; but the story is essentially about the humane and just Negro, Mann, pitted against the injustices and inhumanities of a sadistic Southern white world. In "Long Black Song," Silas eventually comprehends that the steps to financial success in America do not coincide with the steps a Negro must climb in order to reach self-respect and dignity in the eyes of the whole community. In fact, as suggested by one critic, Silas's rejection of the American Dream is really a rejection of bourgeois values; for Silas realizes that the unfaithfulness of his wife, Sarah, may be attributed to a specific aspect of bourgeois codes—that the conquest of a woman is a promiscuous act paralleling the accumulation of wealth and power through unethical, but acceptable, business devices.[28] Furthermore, what intrigues Sarah is a material and superficial object of the new industrial and bourgeois age, a Gramophone. The music emanating from the white man's device creates a dream mood between Sarah's consciousness and subconsciousness that leads to her submission to the white salesman's sexual advances. Finally, the story is framed by two scenes of violence, one merely suggested and the other actually dramatized. Both are an outgrowth of man's inability to cooperate with his fellowman. At the beginning

Sarah, thinking of the boyfriend of her youth, Tom, who was killed in World War I, mentally reflects: "Nothing good could come from men going miles across the seas to fight. N how come they wanna kill each other? . . . Killing was not what men ought to do."[29] At the end Silas's shooting affair with the white posse and his self-immolation by fire in the farmhouse carry back to America, the "native land," the concept of disharmony among men. In both scenes Sarah protectively clutches her daughter, Ruth, perhaps symbolically nursing a new breed to set the world straight. In any event, "Long Black Song" presents a Marxist motif only by extension and implication.

In the final two stories of the collection, "Fire and Cloud" and "Bright and Morning Star," Wright weaves Marxism and the Communist Party into the very fabric of his tales. Although in "Fire and Cloud" Wright denies the Party a major role and presents the two Party members in a shadowy and undeveloped manner, he uses the Great Depression as commentary enough upon the failures of capitalism. When food and relief are cut off from the Negro community by white authorities, the author says as much about the faults of an economic system as he does about racial cruelty and injustice. Preacher Taylor has at one time received the word from God to guide and shepherd his flock, but that world of green pastures and sunny skies he recalls from his past is crumbling around him. The economic realities of the times are shattering his flock's trust in his ability to lead them anywhere. Meanwhile, Chief of Police Bruden, the capitalist stooge in the guise and garb of justice, knows full well that the Party could strike the spark for a blaze of revolt on the part of the Negroes. He also fears an alliance between the blacks and the poor whites. In the most ironic of terms, he warns Taylor against encouraging a protest march through town, suggesting that it would be part of a sinister Communist plot: "I want

you to get this straight! Reds ain't *folks*! Theyre Goddam
. . . rats trying to wreck our country, see? Theyre stirring
up race hate!"[30]

Only after suffering a terrible beating at the hands of
white vigilantes is Preacher Taylor able to convert his religious zeal into social action, to change the "real" in his
life from God to people: "Its the *people*!" he says to his
son. "Theys the ones whut mus be real t us! Gawds wid
the people! . . . We cant hep ourselves er the people when
wes alone."[31] Thus the march is headed by Taylor; poor
whites join ranks with the Negroes; and the first step toward
salvation through social mass action is undertaken, even
though the inspiration for the Negroes must be derived
from the godfather Taylor, rather than from Party workers.
However, the rise of a leader from oppressive capitalistic
circumstances seems in keeping both with Marxism and
the ideology of the Popular Front adopted by the Party
in the second half of the 1930s. Wright here, as in certain
of his poems, is portraying how the consciousness of the
masses may be aroused to action against a system that has
created a lower class, the parallel to a working class.
Racial conflict remains a special problem, but Wright implies that despite it a unity against the prevailing economic
system can be achieved between the two races, even if
the precise methods for shaping such a coalition remain
undescribed in "Fire and Cloud."

The concept of militant and faithful sacrifice by urban
workers is treated better by Wright in "Bright and Morning Star" than in any of his other stories. The theme of
racial conflict is intended to be subsidiary to that of class
conflict. So strongly did Wright himself feel that the story
is more about Marxism than about Negro-white relations
that he wrote in a letter prefaced to a reprint edition by
International Publishers: "Frankly, it is not my story; it
belongs to the workers. I would never have written it

unless I had felt that I had a workers' audience to read it."[32] In any event, although in "Bright and Morning Star" scenes of sadistic white cruelties against Negroes are drawn in vivid and harsh detail and the conclusion pictures the violence of race against race, the emphasis is upon the path to dignity and Marxist salvation taken by Sue, Johnny-Boy's mother. She has already seen one son rushed off to jail for his activities as a Party union organizer near Memphis. Now that she has only one surviving son—for the jailed son, Sug, is no longer thought of as a living entity by Sue—she must take all motherly precautions to save Johnny-Boy from a similar fate. She fears that Johnny-Boy's association with, and activities for, the Party will lead him also to jail or even death. Thus she is initially created by Wright as a symbol of those who would interfere with the work of the Party out of selfish emotional motivations.

Complicating the thrust of the story is the presence of a white girl, Reva, who loves Johnny-Boy and is close to Sue. However, Sue's ultimate identification with the Party occurs not through Reva. Rather, it emerges from both a motherly protective instinct and her reactions to the white deputies who rough-handedly try to extort information from her concerning the whereabouts of her son. Also, because she had trustingly supplied a list of local Party members to a white man, Booker, a new entrant into the Party ranks, and then from Reva has discovered that Booker is not to be trusted, Sue must expiate this error through real action or symbolic gesture. Somehow—Wright fails to provide sufficient motivation—her earlier maternal instincts to protect her son from the danger of the white sheriff and white vigilantes are transformed into a desire to assist the cause of the organization in which her son so fearlessly believes. Somehow her actions at the end of the story, when she shoots Booker at the scene of her son's torture, are bound up in her immediate reactions to the extortion attempt by the sheriff and his men: "Yuh didn't git whut yuh wanted! she thought. . . . N yuh aint gonna *never* git it! Hotly something ached in her to make them feel the intensity of her pride and freedom."[33]

Although Sue's conversion to the side of the Party is influenced by many elements, and certainly does not stem from a knowledge of and a belief in the Marxist dialectic, it is a process related to the words *pride* and *freedom*; it becomes a form of self-respect and dignity that Wright attempts to extend far beyond the patterns of a mother-son relationship. Thus when Sue sees Johnny-Boy undergoing severe physical tortures and yet, out of his militant loyalty to the Party, not revealing any of its plans and secrets, she does not interfere with the brutal proceedings. She instead awaits Booker's appearance. He enters and she shoots him. Of course, Sue has committed a willful act of suicide, but she has also performed the dramatic, symbolic gesture that both expiates an error and creates a unity between her maternal identification with Johnny-Boy and her present enlistment in the services of the Party. For the workers whom Wright wanted to move to action through the story, the message is obvious: if the proletariat desires the freedom and dignity it deserves, it must be prepared to sacrifice its life for the cause. And, as Sue breathes her last, having herself been shot by her son's torturers and killers, Wright provides her with a reward that serves as a symbolic prediction for the future: "Focused and pointed she was, buried in the depths of her star, swallowed in its peace and strength; and not feeling her flesh growing cold, cold as the rain that fell from the invisible sky upon the doomed living and the dead that never dies."[34]

Wright's short stories of the 1930s begin as a portrayal of depressing Southern Negro experiences. In "Bright and Morning Star" they are concluded in a fusion of a regional racial problem, religious motifs, sermonic rhetoric, and poetic devices—combined in a manner suggestive of the ending in James Joyce's "The Dead"; but Wright turns them to political use for the Marxist cause.

Wright's first piece of extended nonfiction is a pictorial folk history of the American Negro, *12 Million Black Voices*. Its prose is generally poetic, and the book is an admirable artistic achievement in both its language and its selection of photographs. In simple and moving words and in diction utilizing poetic devices, Wright fittingly accompanies the numerous emotion-evoking photographs with an appropriate style. The book is his finest display of careful and disciplined writing. The ideas too are masterfully manipulated, around a quasi-Marxist interpretation of Negro-American history. Wright alters the traditional Marxist historical triad—the rigid progression from feudalism to capitalism to socialism—to conform to what he thinks are the complexities of his people's history. He endows his account of the three-hundred-year history with a sense of immediacy through a consistent use of the present verb tense. By so doing, he implies that no distinct time periods can be applied to those three hundred years. In other words, the accounts of a feudalistic society in the first two parts of the book—"Our Strange Birth" and "Inheritors of Slavery"—are not intended to be historically separated from the accounts of the capitalistic urban societies described in Part Three, "Death on the City Pavements." Thus Wright's use of Marxist ideas is less rigid, more fluid, than the ideas themselves. Furthermore, he is able to cope with two important phenomena of the twentieth-century South: the persistent existence of feudallike attitudes and relationships in rural areas and the introduction of modern machinery and industrial productive methods in those same areas. His technique is related as much to his self-identity as a Negro as to an acceptance of Marxism in general.

In 1937, commenting on what he thought a plan for Negro writing should be, Wright proposed Marxism as only a starting point to lay bare the "skeleton of society." The Negro writer should then "plant flesh upon those bones out of his will to live."[35] Accordingly, he felt that a theme would emerge when Negro writers would begin to feel "the meaning of the history of their race as though they in one life time had lived it themselves throughout all the long centuries."[36] Obviously then, Wright recognized American Negro history to be unique, different perhaps from anything that could be placed comfortably within the framework of a Marxist explanation. At the same time, though, he seemed to have found the Marxist emphasis on a society of classes and class struggle appealing for purposes of defining the economic structure and relationships within society. The problem he encountered is an age-old one for the Marxist Parties around the world: how can the existence of a peasant, agricultural class—the majority groups in such lands as Russia and China—be reconciled to historical imperatives that had placed the responsibility for social upheaval and revolution in the hands of the urban proletariat? For Wright the answer was formulated through the selection of the present verb tense to carry historical actions and events. The present time became merely a metaphor for all periods of the past. In this way, he could account for the exceptions that did not fit so snugly into a Marxist superstructure.

From the opening paragraph of *12 Million Black Voices* —which mentions the black folk "upon the dusty land of the farms or upon the hard pavement of the city streets"— to the last, Wright makes a conscious attempt to apply Marxist concepts to an interpretation of American Negro life, past and present, regardless of how far he has to stretch in time and space.[37] He accounts for one aspect of the unique American social structure by placing all Negroes socially and psychologically below whites, but within terminology that echoes of Marxism. Wright asserts that there are three classes of men above the Negro: "the Lords of the Land—operators of the plantations; the Bosses of the Buildings—the owners of industry; and the vast numbers of poor white workers—our immediate competitors in the daily struggle for bread."[38] Although Marxism tries to explain history and society in terms of classes, not races, Wright apparently finds such an uncomplicated rendering not simple enough. He, in fact, does not start with Marxism—as he had earlier urged his fellow Negro writers to do—but instead begins with assumptions related to his perception of a racial schism in American society. By writing about all Negroes, he also includes those blacks who would be quickly placed into a bourgeois category under elementary Marxist precepts. Although Wright concentrates his commentary most strongly on black people who are exploited economically, at the same time by implication his folk history embraces an entire race, which, Wright suggests, is exploited in areas not wholly economic. His vision, of course, represents a rather unorthodox Marxism.

12 Million Black Voices outlines the movement of Negro-American history accurately enough, though the book makes no claim to be a precise, annotated survey. The early history, leading up to the slave trade and to the introduction of Negroes in large numbers to the New World, Wright describes in Marxist terms as an outgrowth of a feudalistic economic situation. Citing man's attempts to overcome nature and to mold natural resources into useful forms, he portrays the European enslavers of the Negro as men escaping from "fetid medieval dens, . . . doffing the burial sheets of feudal religion, and flushed with a new

and noble concept of life, of its inherent dignity, of its un-
limited possibilities."[39] Extending his interpretation quickly
beyond the eighteenth century, Wright contends that America was divided into two worlds, one of machines and the
other of slaves. Out of this process arose two groups of
leaders, whom he names "the Bosses of the Buildings" and
"the Lords of the Land." From the Civil War to World
War I, Wright focuses his account upon the Southern
rural experience (in the lengthy "Inheritors of Slavery"
section). Here he stresses the same kinds of injustices and
violence that he had fictionalized earlier in his short stories.
He stretches this Southern experience beyond any precise date or period for the transformation of the South from
a feudal by-product society into a capitalistic one. This
experience seems to have defied a strict inclusion within
the pure Marxist dialectic.

Wright then treats the Negro migrations to the industrial cities of the North during and after World War I, as
well as the increasing replacement of farm labor with trac-
tors, combines, and other machines on Southern farms and
plantations. Yet he does not suspend in time the reality of
an existing semifeudal social configuration in the South.
When he reaches his conclusion in *12 Million Black Voices*,
he talks not about the "collective hands" of a proletariat;
rather, he merely mentions action on the part of "disciplined, class-conscious groups," then narrows his view
to race-consciousness, the Negro recollection of black
parents, the slavery of grandparents, even the African origins of the race.[40] Thus, though he carries history through
a change from feudalism to capitalism, he strikes a subjective, emotional chord of race rather than the more objective Marxist one of class. By analogizing "the Lords
of the Land" to "the Bosses of the Buildings," he can hope
to inspire active dissent among the poor black farmers of
the South. He can also appeal to both the actual frustra-

tions and the possible Jungian-type memory processes within the Northern urban black masses, whose roots are in the Southern rural soil.

The environment portrayed in "Death on the City Pavements," the last section of *12 Million Black Voices*, takes us into the urban world of *Lawd Today* and *Native Son*. By placing Negroes into the crowded, filthy tenements of the Northern industrial cities, Wright, of course, fits them into a context of advanced capitalism. He persistently points out the exploitation of blacks by whites, whether the whites be workers or union organizers. He also subsumes the evils of racial conflict within the larger evils caused by capitalism: "the majority of black and white . . . live under the spell wrought by the Bosses of the Buildings," or "the Bosses of the Buildings are the generals who decree the advance or retreat."[41]

It appears, then, that Wright's last prolonged piece that favorably uses Marxist materials transcends the subject of racial conflict in America more than any of his previous works, with the possible exception of a few of his early poems—despite the fact that *12 Million Black Voices* centers on the sad history of the American Negro. Paradoxically, Wright cannot unfold that history without underscoring another fact: the strict Marxist dialectic must be altered by the artist-historian so that it can accommodate the racial nature of American-Negro history, not its class structure. In a sense, *12 Million Black Voices* is the symbolic rendering of a political-philosophical dilemma so evidently protruding from the pages of *Lawd Today* and *Native Son*, Wright's two novels written during his Communist Party period. In both works, the Negro artist primarily shouts his protest against racial injustice and prejudice. Secondarily, he attempts to superimpose upon his plots and major themes the tenets of a seemingly useful and "rational" motivation for his protest; that is to say, Wright's head seems to have been vying with his heart. In *12 Million Black Voices*—an emotional piece really—his heart wins, at the expense of a rigid and "rational" Marxist dialectic. That Wright's position in the Party was shaky is not surprising.

An earlier Marxist-influenced work is *Lawd Today*, but to call it a proletarian novel would be a distortion. Instead, it is a study of depravity and deprivation during a single representative day in the life of a Negro in Chicago's Black Belt. Its thematic material makes it a protest novel, one which seeks by extension an end to white racial superiority and bias. It seeks to help in inspiring a swift and permanent removal of the conditions and attitudes creating the frustrated and degraded personalities of all the black Jake Jacksons in their ugly and rancid Black Belts. *Lawd Today* does not openly advocate the Marxist revolution as the solution, but Marxism and the Communist Party survive the novel as unexplored possibilities for hope and salvation, even though they have been battered and beleaguered by the clichés of Jake and his friends. Unlike the later *Native Son*, *Lawd Today* assumes on the part of its reading audience a knowledge of both Marxism and the expressed aims of the American Communist Party. Although scenes and speeches in the novel that are literally anti-Marxist are balanced with none that are literally pro-Marxist, the anti-Marxist materials are planted in such a way as to appeal to the reader's ironic sense and to evoke from him a sympathy for a Marxist solution to racial problems. Nevertheless, the reader is never able to forget that the subject of the novel is black men in a white world, not workers in a capitalistic world. There is no assurance that even if the Marxist revolution were to fire and transform America, racial conflict would subside and then swoon in a predictable death. Instead, there seems to be only a possible hope

—the attitude already infiltrating Wright's proletarian poetry at this time.

The Chicago setting in *Lawd Today* parallels the pictorial settings in the last section of *12 Million Black Voices*, where scene after scene is snapped along big-city pavements in the slums. Although "the Bosses of the Buildings" are neither heard nor seen in *Lawd Today*, they can be sensed lurking in the shadows of naturalistic word-paintings created by Wright in the different locales of the Black Belt—Jake and Lil's depressingly drab apartment, Doc Higgins's Tonsorial Parlor, the Calumet Avenue dance hall. Serving as a motif is an undercurrent of financial exploitation, which is intensified when Jake must borrow money from a fellow post-office worker at an exorbitant interest rate, after he has already saved his job by paying Doc Higgins a one-hundred-and-fifty-dollar fee for bribing his city-hall connections. Of course, on a more significant level—one related to white dominance—the novel is about the exploitation and the stifling of personality; but economic exploitation, which both cuts across racial lines and operates within racial groups, is also a vital theme throughout this work. In fact, Jake and his friends move in a world in which personality is often defined by money —or at least that is the concept by which they understand reality outside of a racial context. When Jake reads about President Roosevelt's "attack" on banks, he reflects that "cold, hard cash runs this country, always did and always will." Furthermore, he feels that "nobody'll ever tell these rich American men what to do."[42] Suggested here is a contention held during the early depression years by the Communist Party that President Roosevelt either could not or did not intend to control the power of banking interests, the Party's archenemies and a prime target of the revolution. Beyond this specific reference is the general idea that money and society are synonymous. At this point it would appear that Jake shares the insights of the Marxists about an evil within the capitalistic system; however, we soon see that Jake is a victim of capitalistic indoctrination. One of the frustrations in his life is his inability to acquire the money that he equates with power.

Wright's emphasis on money in *Lawd Today* may simply be interpreted as an attempt to focus attention upon the absence of human values in the lives of Jake and his friends; it also fortifies the concept that the Northern urban Negro has become a pawn of financial forces, even though his environment does not pose the same threat of personal physical violence present in the rural South. However, the novel's concern with money is validly associated with that unexamined social and economic alternative, the Marxist revolution, which hides behind the ironic implications of many scenes.

Wright portrays only a single Communist in the novel; he is seen once and hardly speaks a word. A few minutes before he is encountered by Jake, Jake has been reading a newspaper report of a riot in the streets of New York that was apparently Communist inspired. Jake's reaction needs little interpretive assistance to make clear the obvious and loud ironic note:

Now them guys, them Commoonists and Bolshehicks, is the craziest guys going! They don't know what they want. They done come 'way over here and wants to tell us how to run *our* country when their *own* country ain't run right. . . . Why don't they stay in their own country if they don't like the good old U.S.A.? . . . and they go around fooling folks, telling 'em they going to divide up everything. And some folks ain't got no better sense than to believe it, neither.[43]

The reference to "*our* country" pertains to the American black man, who is an alien in his own country. It also extends, within the political context of the newspaper article and of Jake's reaction, to the realm of the dispossessed and exploited masses, skin colors irrelevant, so integral to the successes of Marxist revolutions. Here Wright attempts a fusion of racial problems and socio-class solutions, employing the same techniques that Communist propaganda has often used in its appeal to the American Negro. This particular passage, as it stands isolated from the rest of *Lawd Today*, seems to accomplish the author's intentions much better than does the novel as a whole. Coming as it does so early in the plot, it manages to introduce solidly the subject of Marxism and the Communist Party as a possible means of action for some dissidents. As the story proceeds, in all its drabness of setting and of dialogue, there is little doubt that Jake should be categorized with those who have cause to cry and act for change.

At Doc Higgins's Tonsorial Parlor, Jake enters at the end of a verbal argument between Doc and Duke, the Negro Communist. Jake steps into the spat and chastises Duke: "Why can't you *red* niggers get some sense in your heads? Don't you know them Reds is just using you?" Then Jake moves away from the topic of the Negro as Communist and imagines Doc as the satisfied, secure, and important bourgeois success: "Look at the Doc here! He's a race man! A precinct captain. A businessman. A property owner. He's got pull with all the big politicians in the Loop. . . . Doc's setting pretty; why don't you play the game?"[44]

Later that day, the same Doc will ask Jake for a seventy-five-dollar fee to help save Jake's job and then will charge one-hundred-and-fifty dollars when he finds that Jake has no other sources of money or influence. Here Wright obviously links together money, the capitalistic system, and the Negro in a white-dominated world. Although a sense of corruption and exploitation cuts through two racial worlds, the Communist Negro is left free from taint. Wright then drops the Party worker from the novel, hoping perhaps that the image of Duke and Marxism will be retained as a happy substitute for Jake's one-day journey through the bleak horror of his urban capitalistic environment. As Duke exits, Jake and Doc continue to discuss him. Jake affirms that "colored folks ought to stick with the rich white folks," emulating Booker T. Washington's advice to "cooperate and get along." As for Duke, Jake says that he should heed Washington's words too, "instead of running around here talking about overthrowing the government."[45] Again, the irony is intended for the reader and eludes the speaker's perception.

After introducing the subject of Marxism early, Wright suspends direct allusions to it until one brief passage beyond the midpoint in *Lawd Today*. Repeatedly he inserts conversations among Jake and his friends without identifying the speakers. One effect of this method is the creation of a sense of conformity in thought and speech among the men. By employing this technique associated with the proletarian pluralistic novel, Wright suggests an anonymity and a sameness in the characters, which may represent an actual or a subsconscious bond among the members of a social class, usually the working class:

"Ain't it funny how some few folks is rich and just millions is poor?"

"And them few rich folks owns the whole world. . . ."

". . . and runs it like they please. . . ."

". . . and the rest ain't got nothing?"

"Well, you know Gawd said the poor'll be with you always. . . ."

". . . and He was right, too."[46]

Here the novel transcends protest over a specific issue. It deals with general social justice, while still using the recurrent image of money. Only a short time later, in the conversation among the men, the talk centers around the hopeless future for the Negro postal workers in particular, and American Negroes in general. What begins as a racial subject is elevated progressively but unconsciously among the men to the thematic dimension of class identity and consciousness, needing only the timely injection of Marxist leadership to transform suppressed anger into organized revolutionary activity:

"But things can't go on like this always."

". . . I wish there was a man somewhere who knowed how to lead. . . ."

"There'll be a man like that some day. . . ."

". . . and things start to change then."

". . . For something like that I wouldn't mind fighting and dying. . . ."

". . . Now, you see, if *all* folks felt like that, why in hell don't they *do* something?"

"Aw, hell! Some guy's got something *you* want, and you got something *he* wants, and when you start to do something you bump into each other. . . ."

"Yeah, like you see trains crashing up in the movies."

"But, shucks, if we all was in the same train going in the same direction. . . ."[47]

"The same train going in the same direction"—after this image Wright drops all overt allusions to the Marxist theme. From here the men do move in the same direction: they are sucked deeper into the muck of their Black Belt existence. They channel their frustrations into the smoke- and jazz-filled dance-hall den of prostitution, liquor, and narcotics. On one level of the novel's meaning, they can make no connection between their blighted Negro life and the radio speeches heard throughout the day commemorating Lincoln's birthday. On another, less persistent level, they are the fallen angels from whom the vanguards of the Marxist revolution could have been molded.

Lawd Today is artistically unappealing for many reasons, but Wright's method of inserting the Marxist motif shows an admirable skill. The unobtrusiveness, subtlety, and irony with which these particular socio-politico-economic materials are handled are, in fact, especially commendable in the light of how Wright later uses Marxism in the last section of his larger and generally finer novel *Native Son.*

In *Native Son* direct references to Marxism and the Party are introduced sporadically in the early part of the book. From the outset Wright emphasizes the poor living conditions in the Black Belt, aptly underlined by the opening description of the crowded, ugly, Thomas apartment and by the depiction of Bigger's rat chase. The scene then shifts outside to the Black Belt, revealing much of the same dreary, depressing, run-down city landscape as in *Lawd Today.* Later, Bigger advances to the Northside area of private and opulent homes, a distinct contrast to the antiquated slum setting of his Negro existence. His employer, Mr. Dalton, happens to own the very building in which the Thomas apartment is located. The rent, of course, is exorbitant. Furthermore, Mr. Dalton has periodically converted his profits from the rents into magnanimous contributions to various Negro institutions. At this point Wright establishes a circular connection easily accounted for by "objective" Marxist historians: under the spell of the profit motive, the bourgeois capitalists drain off the hard-earned wages of their laboring-class underlings; then, with public fanfare, they restore a portion of their high profits to the exploited, in order to discourage revolt and to appease their own feelings of guilt. At the center of the circle are the capitalists' propaganda machines, supported by another slice of bourgeois profits to maintain the fiction of economic success through individual, honest assertion and hard work, unrestrained by the strangling fetters of governmental control. In the case of Mr. Dalton, Wright specifically highlights white hyprocrisy.

The technical and aesthetic problem that Wright has to

face in planting such Marxist materials in *Native Son* is
how to accomplish it with both force and subtlety. Employing a device used earlier in *Lawd Today*, he mentions communism near the beginning of the novel and depicts his
Negro characters' ignorance about and prejudice against
the Party. He also shows that the source of information
about, and of the feeling against, Marxism in general and
the Party in particular is the mass media. When Bigger
and the members of his gang watch a movie in which a
Communist—the evil figure in the movie's plot—hurls a
bomb at innocent people, they whisper among themselves
their ignorant beliefs that "a red" is "a race of folks who
live in Russia," who "must be wild" because their representative on the screen is irresponsibly "trying to kill somebody."[48] Soon thereafter, in the early moments of his brief
associations with Mary Dalton and Jan Erlone, Bigger is
allowed to voice his conception of Marxists, uninformed
as Wright intends it to be:

And what were Communists like, anyway? . . . What made
people Communists? He remembered seeing many cartoons
of Communists in newspapers and always they had flaming
torches in their hands and wore beards and were trying
to commit murder or set things on fire. . . . All he could
recall . . . about Communists was associated in his mind with
darkness, old houses, people speaking in whispers, and
trade unions on strike.[49]

Thus the Marxist motif is quickly infused. Here, as in
Lawd Today, Wright gains an ironic effect by making inac-
curate and absurd the anti-Communist conceptions on the
part of society's exploited members, who have been both
indoctrinated and victimized.

With the appearance of Jan Erlone, the young Party
worker who is also Mary Dalton's boyfriend, the novel becomes blatantly propagandistic. On one level, Jan represents the first white man who has been friendly to Bigger.

On another level, he embodies the faithful worker who spreads the Marxist gospel and the Party's propaganda among all oppressed peoples. Jan's dual role is part of Wright's attempt to superimpose what appears to be a larger and more rational solution upon the American racial conflict, which itself is the result of historical forces not so easily explained or, for that matter, solved through the projections of the rigid Marxist interpretation of history. The fact that throughout the novel Jan remains an undeveloped, insufficiently motivated figure may indicate either that Wright could not fully believe the probability that racially unprejudiced whites do exist, or that he could not deal convincingly with white or white-Communist psychology. In any case, he allows Bigger to exploit for his own benefit the unfavorable and reactionary predispositions that Wright thought most Americans held toward Marxists during the 1930s.

After Mary Dalton's death and incineration, Bigger connives to implicate Jan in Mary's strange disappearance from the Dalton household. Both the police and the newspapermen jump to conclusions from the fabricated story told them by Bigger, whom they regard as a stupid but well-meaning and honest Negro. They quickly prejudge the Marxist Jan, and he is held in jail. Taking advantage of the public's attitude toward the Party, Bigger pens a ransom note demanding ten thousand dollars for Mary's return, signing the note "Red" above a drawing of the hammer-and-sickle emblem of the Party. Thus, for a portion of the novel, the Communist Party is thrust upon the reader as a much-maligned and abused force. However, in terms of the black-white problems of America, as they are focused in the story of Bigger Thomas, the Party serves as the friend of the Negro. Wright implies that the Party is the unexplored hope for a solution to the larger and broader social and economic issues of the country.

Wright's treatment of the Marxist materials in the first two sections of *Native Son* is much the same as in the whole of *Lawd Today*, although the inclusion of Jan in *Native Son* accentuates the Marxist motif more strongly. In both novels the concept of salvation through a Marxist revolution is held above the plots as an uninvestigated alternative to a social and economic system that exploits Negro labor and personality. In both, too, the main Negro figures and their cronies are depicted as the uninformed but innocent foes of their possible salvation. Wright does establish early in both novels that the Negro characters are searching in their own half-hearted, unguided manner for some type of plan or leadership to capture the unconscious emotions of all black people and direct them to a willed, dignified, and better fate. Like Jake Jackson and his friends, Bigger wishes, after his initial contact with Jan, that Negroes could be welded into an active body moving in a single coordinated stride: "Dimly, he felt that there should be one direction in which he and all other black people could go whole-heartedly; that there should be a way in which gnawing hunger and restless aspiration could be fused; that there should be a manner of acting that caught the mind and body in certainty and faith."[50] Bigger is then moved to an admiration of Hitler and Mussolini, historical tyrants who have whipped together nations of disparate elements into powerful world forces; he also refers to the Spanish civil war. By this allusion to fascism, Wright suggests that dissidents can be bound together in meaningful mass action.

In the courtroom scene in the novel's final section, entitled "Fate," Bigger's lawyer Max is engaged in two projects: to win Bigger's confidence and faith in him and his political beliefs, and to direct to the judge a plea that will expose capitalism as the root of Bigger's unpremeditated crime. In the end, there is still the question whether Bigger has been influenced by anything more than Max's open display of fatherly friendship; however, the judge is clearly convinced that Bigger himself, not the capitalistic system, is guilty of a crime. Through Max, Wright undoubtedly is attacking capitalism and offering in its place the vision of a brighter, happier society.

One sampling of Max's speech is sufficient to demonstrate the Party line that Wright takes at the end of the novel. Max explains for the court how and why a latent hate has been fanned in the jury and among the crowd that mingles in the streets outside the court building. Linking bankers, the Manufacturers' Association, the governor, the mayor, the state's attorney, city merchants, and state militiamen, that is, the gamut of organizations and institutions that are the entrenched enemies of the proletariat, Max proclaims: "All of them—the mob and the mob masters; the wire-pullers and the frightened; the leaders and their pet vassals—know and feel that their lives are built upon a historical deed of wrong against many people, people from whose lives they have bled their leisure and their luxury!"[51]

With Max and the courtroom scene, Wright handles his Marxist materials less appropriately than the manner in which he had treated them in *Lawd Today*. However, he never admitted in print that the insistent inclusion of Max's speech near the end of the novel was inappropriate or overdone. In fact, one of his strongest public avowals of communism was in a response to a review by David L. Cohn that attacked, among other things, the Marxist antidote for Bigger's and America's ills.[52] Proclaimed Wright: "The Negro problem . . . is *not* beyond solution. . . . I am proletarian and Mr. Cohn is bourgeois; we live on different planes of social reality." Expanding the content of Max's courtroom plea, Wright then urged all Negroes "to become strong through *alliances*, by joining in common cause with other oppressed groups . . . , workers, *sensible* Jews . . .

and so forth."[53] The didacticism of the final section in *Native Son* seems then to have been intended to be just that, and presumably it was meant to contribute to the artistic unity of the novel. However, intention and effect do not always correspond, and it is precisely the divergence of the two that detracts from the sense of unequivocal achievement for *Native Son*.

It is not Marxism as such that detracts from the themes of the novel; in fact, a Marxist interpretation does provide a useful tool for partially explaining the sociological and economic backgrounds for American Negro-white relations. Instead, Wright's emphasis on socio-politico-economic explanations of Bigger's predicament causes an undesirable shift in focus from the fascinating personal story of Bigger's psychological life. Bigger's problems revolve around the concept of relatedness to other people—black and white—and to institutions; his struggle is for love and trust in a hostile environment, not for a socio-politico-economic ideology.[54] Beyond the perimeters of racial conflict, historical interpretations, and political beliefs, Bigger's psyche has been constructed by Wright as an intriguing amalgam of nihilistic and existential ideas; and Bigger may be regarded as a prototype for the nihilistic-existential protagonist of *The Outsider*, Cross Damon. True, *Native Son* is unquestionably a better novel than *Lawd Today* because of Wright's ability to sustain a powerful and compelling simple narrative around the consciousness of his main Negro figure. True, too, *Native Son* probably will continue to be considered a milestone in the history of American social fiction, but Wright's heavy-handed manipulation of his Marxist materials will tend to stand in the way of favorable aesthetic judgments.

In *The Outsider*, Cross Damon, a Negro, is isolated and alienated from other men *because* he is a man.[55] The novel is one of the few examples in American fiction of an author's conscious attempt to shape existential themes. The work also offers an unflattering commentary on the Communist Party. In many respects, and especially in its treatment of the Party, *The Outsider* may be compared to Ralph Ellison's *Invisible Man* (1952), published only a few months before Wright's novel. One striking parallel between Ellison's unnamed central narrator and Cross Damon is their search for identity beyond the context of racial conflict. In both works it is the Party that feels it can provide a basis for identity, and in both novels it is the Party that exploits the fact of the main figure's color, for political and propagandistic gain. In terms of the Marxist content in *The Outsider* (the wider existential themes are analyzed in Chapter 4), the Party's treatment of Cross Damon clearly echoes words set down by Wright in a 1945 publication, only months after his formal break with the Party, but years before he wrote *The Outsider*: "Both the political Left and the political Right try to change the Negro problem into something that they can control, thereby denying the humanity of the Negro, excluding his unique and historic position in American life."[56] This attitude is essentially the basis for Wright's attack on the Party in *The Outsider*. It reflects the position that he had taken earlier in his essay in *The God That Failed*.

In *The Outsider*, a novel of violence in the form of senseless murders, Wright allows Cross Damon to act out the inhumane prerogatives embodied within Cross's nihilistic-existential philosophy. Wright does include a long tract-like section that is intended to explain to the reader the beliefs controlling the narrative. The aesthetic purpose of this inclusion is dubious, although the political and philosophical themes are clarified.

Having killed an innocent fellow postal worker in Chicago and a fascist landlord and two Communists in New

York, and having so far escaped detection, Cross Damon engages Blimin, the Party dialectician, in a tense dialogue. In a speech too long and too filled with complex logic to be realistic, even though the scene itself is created realistically, Cross applies a Marxist interpretation to history. He accounts for modern industrialism and capitalistic exploitation, but explains that industrialization "could have been accomplished under a dozen different ideological banners." He calls dialectical materialism in Russia only one of many possible, and equally valid, approaches to an industrialized state. He condemns the Russian Marxists as "a small group of ruthless men" who "seized power and . . . established a dictatorship." The dictatorship, he feels, owes its success to its ability to maintain fictions and myths in a world that science is rationalizing, and in which a combination of science and industrialism has already sheared man away from a belief in God. In God's place remains a mythical void to be filled by the super-perceivers desiring power. Of Blimin and the Marxists, Cross claims: "You use idealistic words as your smoke screen, but behind that screen you *rule.* . . . It's a question of *power!*" The revolutionary is, he thinks, "a cold kind" of thinker who possesses "a sense of what power is, what it's for." He has one aim, "direct and naked power!" Cross then argues that the Marxists are no different from the fascists in their desire and program for power, but that the Marxists do have an initial advantage by proffering an ideology appealing even to men who are most alienated from the mythical fictions of their cultures.[57]

Cross Damon has recognized "the truth" of his own alienation. He resents being manipulated by an organization that, for the enhancement of its own power, will exploit what he contends is the fact of man's alienation. He thus can justify his own savage destruction of those people who would use him. In the end Cross also dies, unfulfilled by his games of death and deception, thus, of course, negating the worth, in human terms, of his own nihilistic-existential position.

Throughout the melodrama, we wonder how closely the author has identified with his protagonist, just as in reading *Native Son* we are tempted to surmise at what points Bigger Thomas is really Richard Wright. However, with or without a precise discovery of homologous relationships—author to central characters—the reversal in Wright's attitudes toward Marxism and the Communist Party in America is distinct. No doubt the tract-like technique employed in *Native Son* and *The Outsider* to illuminate the authorial bias is aesthetically offensive. The didactic, propagandistic, pro-Marxist nature of Max's speech in *Native Son* tends to limit themes. However, Cross Damon's speech in *The Outsider*, though it is anti-Marxist, suggests a larger metaphysical dimension for motifs and themes. In *Native Son*, Wright seems to be posing a socio-politico-economic salvation for Bigger's psychological and human problems. In *The Outsider*, after Marxism, fascism, and other historical systems have been rejected by Cross, Wright must contend with Cross's basic belief that man is tragically alienated from man.

After 1953, the publication date for *The Outsider*, Wright apparently felt a need to retrace the steps of his own philosophical development, including his odyssey from political ignorance, to Marxist belief, to an anti-Marxist position. In his nonfiction of the last half decade of his life—the European, African, and Asian political journey books to be examined in the next chapter—we learn that though Wright experienced urgent impulses to discuss Marxism as a real force in the larger world of continents of many races and ideas, he remained staunchly anti-Communist. Although in his nonfiction of the 1950s he could not avoid treating, and even dwelling upon, Marxist themes and materials, he shunned all such references in his later novels,

Savage Holiday (1954) and *The Long Dream* (1958), both written in France but narrowed to American settings. In effect, Wright may have been confirming that Marxism and America, let alone Marxism and the American-Negro artist, have not mixed well historically. Wright undoubtedly became convinced that Marxism and the Communist Parties no longer represented his aspiration and vision for a new and better world: "brotherhood, universality, hope of harmony, universal reason and an assumption of natural immutable moral laws."[58]

CHAPTER 3

New Perspectives
Outside America

IN LATE 1945 the provisional French government invited
Wright to visit France. By late 1946, after his trip to France
and a return to New York, Wright decided to make his
home in Paris. Many factors contributed to his decision:
an abiding reservation about the fate of race relations in
America, his marriage to a white woman, a daughter who
he felt was destined to be an outsider in American life, a
suspicion that his past association with the Communist
Party would soon make him persona non grata in his native
land. Certainly, the French reputation for accepting into
their culture and society aliens of any skin color attracted
him.[1] Only once after 1947 did he return to the United
States, and then just briefly.[2]

Wright's years of self-imposed exile in Paris and on his
Normandy farm, from 1947 until his death in 1960, were
not years of withdrawal and isolation. He continued to
write fiction and, near the end of his life, to compose hokku
and "haiku" poetry. Furthermore, he became friendly with
French writers and philosophers, especially the existentialists, and notably Jean-Paul Sartre. Through Sartre and
the other existentialists he probably clarified his own quasi-

existential thinking and discovered the ideas and terms that form a basis for *The Outsider*. His contacts with French intellectuals and thought also helped Wright to extend his sentiments about race and social structures, including Marxism, beyond the boundaries of his American experiences. However, his years away from America provided him with even greater opportunities to enlarge his thinking and to add new subject matter to his writing. As significant in the development of his own ideas and the direction of his prose were his travels to other countries, scattered on different continents. These trips expanded Wright's vision to a world of many races and cultures so that he felt impelled to comment in his nonfiction on what he saw and sensed in such places as Spain, Indonesia, and the African Gold Coast (now Ghana).

As we know from his publications before his move to France, Wright's intellectual focus had been upon the American racial theme and on the Communist Party and Marxism in America. In his main period of nonfiction, concentrated between 1953 and 1957, the general thematic matter shifts little. Important qualifications do appear, however. Not only are Wright's themes of race and politics advanced to the international scene, but his interest in metaphysical definitions for man becomes keener. As a result, in his late long nonfiction he assumes a variety of poses—traveler, interviewing journalist, political scientist, and philosopher.

In his three books involving travel—*Black Power* (1954), *The Color Curtain* (1956), and *Pagan Spain* (1957)—Wright sets out on a journey to undertake an objective analysis of a place, a people, or an event. He informs his reader of the circumstances precipitating his expedition and then reveals the particular knowledge, feelings, and prejudices he had begun with. Through what seems always to be a faithful recording of his interviews with the people he had met, of both low and high station, and of his reactions to places and circumstances, he remains objective. Furthermore, he introduces and periodically uses such documentary sources as history books, political handbooks, and speeches. Because of Wright's technique of asking penetrating and significant questions about his topics, his nonfiction creates the impression that he is seeking fresh viewpoints and answers to be discovered through his objective investigations. However, too often he approaches international problems in a seemingly objective fashion, but then suggests solutions for them by reasserting his prior beliefs. Accordingly, the objectivity sought for in his travels is eroded to some extent by this type of subjectivity. Nevertheless, there are moments when he attains new personal perspectives or when his prior commitments are either reshaped or abandoned.

In areas of major social concerns, such as race, politics, and religion, his conclusions usually do not represent original landmarks in the history of thought and ideas. What he says has been expressed in the past by specialists in political analysis, theological and philosophical investigation, sociological study, and international journalism. Yet, for a broad view of Wright's thinking in the 1950s, it is important to see how he handles the topic of race relations when he comments on areas, far removed from America, where the populations are not predominantly white, and how he treats Marxism as a force in the world, not merely in America. In his journey to other lands, Wright is pressed to take into open account the emotional, religious, and metaphysical factors that he had come to believe were assuming a large part in determining the direction of many international policies and decisions and that, in the case of Spain, had to be understood before Spanish character could be defined. Although Wright's nonfiction of the 1950s may not prove to be the medium by which posterity will best remember him, it is valuable for a full elucidation of the man and of his ideas and opinions.

Perhaps it is in the history of American letters that Wright's nonfiction acquires importance—not necessarily for its content but for its presence. Like some American novelists after World War II—enough in number to imply a trend—he transferred contemporary sociological and political topics from the genre of fiction to that of the extended essay. He had, of course, included long essay-like tracts in certain of his novels, notably *Native Son* and *The Outsider*. Although the value of his art is reduced because of this tendency, his successes in creating dramatic settings and realistic dialogues in his fiction, when added to his earlier indulgence in essay-like forms, aided him in producing travel books that are not merely pedestrian journalism.

Black Power is Wright's first travel book. It portrays the events of his trip to the African Gold Coast in the summer of 1953. At that time the Gold Coast was in the process not only of gaining its independence from Great Britain but of building the political machinery for its self-rule and self-identity under the leadership of the popular Kwame Nkrumah, head of the Convention People's Party. No special occasion had motivated Wright to embark on his tour. After an Easter Sunday luncheon at his Paris apartment, one of his guests suggested that since Wright's desk appeared clear of work, he should go to the Gold Coast, where a new black nation was soon to be born. Wright pondered why such an expedition could be important for him: did he himself possess a racial heritage that placed him in a position to know intuitively what Africa is? Would he be able to perceive connections between his personality and what Western whites had generalized to be the common African traits of the Negro personality? Because of his color and because of a racial heritage that he unconsciously had perhaps retained, would he be able to communicate freely with black strangers on the continent of his ancestors?[3] Throughout *Black Power* similar inwardly directed questions are a unique characteristic of the work. Although Wright's concerns and discussions drift toward history, economics, and politics, at the center of his writings is an acute awareness that many resolutions must germinate from his concentrating on the facts of the real or imagined racial differences and the racial myths that he himself had been exposed to.

In the introductory chapter to *Black Power*, "Apropos Prepossessions," Wright states that two things inspired him to publish an account of his trip: his desires to show the Western world "how hard and inhuman" its face looked to Africans and to provide Westerners with insight into Africa's future.[4] To some extent he accomplishes these purposes, though we should not conclude that his remarks about the Gold Coast can so easily be applied to all of diverse black Africa. Nevertheless, *Black Power* is an author-centered publication, and as such it communicates more than a sense of the political climate and the future of the Gold Coast. Undoubtedly, the objectivity that readers would hope for in a re-creation of a journey to a strange land is undercut, but gained is a sense that we are being drawn into the complexities and perplexities of Wright's mind. An intriguing aspect of the book is that we are allowed to view, as one commentator has pointed out, an American Negro, a professional writer besides, who "confronted Africa with all sorts of harsh and complicated questions in his mind." His reactions were on several different levels, because he surveyed the Gold Coast "as a Western man, a man of Paris, New York, Chicago, a comer to Africa from a different world."[5] As a Negro, he approached Africa, as it unfolded before him, with attitudes and emotions different from those of a white Westerner. Thus the fascinating qualities of *Black Power* lie more in the author than in the external subject, although the idea of Wright as an international political visionary should not be understated.

Black Power quickly reveals Wright's disposition toward and his use of Marxist prepositions. In the introductory section, after mentioning honestly and without embarrassment his past affiliation with the Communist Party, he briefly exposes some of the causes of his disillusionment with the Party. He nevertheless indicates that his presentation of Western history, as it affects Africa, is founded on a Marxist analysis. For those who would object to this type of historical explanation, he maintains that he is sufficiently flexible and willing to "accept any other method of interpreting the facts," but insists that other schemes *"must not exclude the facts!"*[6] Earlier, when he treated American Negro history in *12 Million Black Voices*, Wright had distorted a rigid Marxist explanation by emphasizing the emotional aspects of Negro-white problems that do not fit so easily into a Marxist pattern; but in *Black Power* he apparently is guided by a Marxist interpretation because he has discovered that an inclusion of those matters which suppose racial superiority and awareness would overly complicate his brief account of colonial history. Furthermore, Marxism remained for Wright a useful instrument for analyzing history.

The long sections of Western colonial history scattered throughout *Black Power* are examples of classical Marxist interpretations. Sketched out are the rise of a Western European bourgeois class, the advance of technology, the need for foreign markets and foreign sources of raw materials, and the ensuing conquest and subjugation of colored peoples at the hands of white Western invaders. As usual, the Marxist explanation offers an element of rational and scientific authority. At the same time, it underplays the concepts of European superiority based upon white racial feelings about nonwhites. Accordingly, throughout *Black Power*, Wright strains to shield his apparent belief that the damage inflicted upon the black African personality has occurred through the instruments of white European racial superiority. The culprit ostensibly is colonialism: "Centuries of foreign rule had left their marks deep, deep in the personalities of the people."[7] However, Wright implies in other statements in *Black Power* that the scars had not been imposed solely by the hard forces of the capitalistic segment of history explained by Marx, for racial awareness and superiority had made their own deep penetrations.

To illustrate the racial aspects of African history, Wright supplies incident after incident in which a white Westerner belittles, on purely racial grounds, any constructive black African attempts at organization or production, either political or economic. At these moments, Wright refrains from pointing out the obvious, allowing his white informers, instead, to reveal unwittingly the racial prejudices influencing both the past and the present. For instance, Britishers at a cocktail party need only to refer to the Africans as savages to provide a vivid depiction of a history existing outside a rigid Marxist portrayal. Yet Wright insists that the Britishers are, above all, "cold, astute businessmen"— capitalists, that is—who desire the retention of their position as conqueror in order to maintain their economic advantage.[8] He never firmly states, however, that racial attitudes rest so fixedly within the framework of capitalistic exploitation. A strange duality is thus posed in *Black Power*: on the one hand, as a political commentator, Wright attempts to make his readers view the Gold Coast's past as an adjunct within a capitalistic and class-dominated historical conformation; on the other hand, as a Negro sensitive to centuries of black subjection to white insult and cruelty, he is unable to conceal a personal inclination

—emotional and subjective—to view the history of the Gold Coast in terms of race, not of class.

A journey that owed its conception to racial interests and considerations during a casual Easter Sunday conversation in Paris never sheds the marks of that beginning. As a result, that clash between a Marxist and a racial outlook evident, for instance, in *Native Son* emerges again, almost a decade and a half later, in *Black Power*. In the novel the effects are aesthetically displeasing, perhaps more because of Wright's method of blunt implantation of Marxist materials than from the appearance of a divided authorial allegiance. In *Black Power* the results are not so disconcerting, for, although Wright cannot decide which of the two elements has primacy, he is working within a genre that does not depend so much as a novel does for its success on a consistent treatment of its thematic materials. Furthermore, the history with which he is dealing may very well be more complex than a single and strict interpretation would make it out to be.

If Wright's account of the history of the African Gold Coast reflects a vacillating center of consciousness, his observations on the conditions in the Gold Coast in the 1950s and his suggestions for that land's future do not. In the first place, after setting down interviews with numerous Africans from the coast to the extremes of the northern hinterlands—including some with Nkrumah—Wright concludes that what he saw there was not communism, for communism is a matter of ideology. The political trends he witnessed were motivated essentially by "the quintessence of passion."[9] Secondly, Wright claims with conviction that an acceptance of assistance from the Soviet Union would lead only to a different kind of subservience and colonialism. Characteristically enough, in a public letter to Nkrumah, he couched his references to Communist Russia in terms of a racial sensitivity: "Why should you change one set of white masters for another?"[10] Obviously, Wright found the Marxist interpretation of history useful when it was applied to the past only, even if the history of racial issues fostered ideological complications. However, as in *The Outsider*, published just months before his trip to the Gold Coast, Wright's outlook in *Black Power* represents a distrust of the real power configurations that have arisen in time out of pure ideology. In another sense, *Black Power* underlines the broader terms in which he was willing in the 1950s to discuss current political matters. No example but the open letter to Nkrumah can better illustrate this change in direction of Wright's political thinking. The letter is a final commentary and pronouncement on Wright's safari to Africa. It projects the author as a man who is saintly optimistic about the future of black African nationalism, but who is also soberly aware of the harsh and impersonal political policies that might have to accompany African advances into the international power scheme. The authorial posture is enigmatic.

The letter to Nkrumah focuses upon the present, and Wright's recommendations are guided by a number of prepositions. The first is that the Gold Coast people have had their psychic growth stunted by the oppressive policies of the ruling colonialists. Therefore, before these people can move from a tribal order to a twentieth-century order, they must establish a sense of confidence. Although Wright does not clarify precisely how to achieve this confidence, he claims that a reorganization of economic power will not be sufficient in itself. However, the sense of confidence must come from within the country, not from the West. Wright then asks Nkrumah to assume benevolent control of the Gold Coast, asserting, though, "*You must be hard!*" There will be suffering, he admits, but he pleads with Nkrumah to "impose it upon *one* generation," and not through a ruthless and rigid adherence to a single economic and political doctrine. The practices must be pragmatic: "You've got to find your *own* paths, your *own* values. . . . Above all, feel free to *improvise!*" The "stagnancy of tribalism" should be overcome so that a new social discipline based on pride and hard work might arise. The key to progress toward this goal is—Wright nearly shouts —"AFRICAN LIFE MUST BE MILITARIZED!" To appease critics who might feel that such actions smack of communism, fascism, or nazism, Wright places trust in Nkrumah and other leaders that they will not form a military dictatorship. Instead, the militarization of African life must be "not for war, but for peace; not for destruction, but for service; not for aggression, but for production; not for despotism, but to free minds from mumbo-jumbo." Meanwhile, Wright claims neither the West nor Russia should be trusted, for "they'll pounce at any time upon Africa to solve their own hard-pressing social and political problems."[11]

Wright's remarks are general and do not outline for Nkrumah and the Gold Coast a set of specific procedures. They are sufficiently full, however, to confirm in Wright's thinking a shift away from a reliance on purely Marxist medicines for social and economic ills. In fact, Wright seemed to be renewing certain American political traditions. He assumed that in the near future a democratic and just society would be achieved through pragmatic devices formulated by responsible public officials. He further assumed that rule by men would be replaced gradually with rule by law. The obvious weakness in Wright's political perspective was the lack of built-in controls and checks to halt a dictatorship. A possible outcome of Wright's outline would be a political system similar to those emerging from early postrevolutionary conditions in Communist countries—a consequence Wright vehemently despised. In all fairness, though, we must note that Wright was not calling for outright government control and ownership of the means of production. To this extent, he unbound himself from Marxist economic presuppositions, without finding, however, an adequate substitute for a dialectical interpretation of African colonial history.

Ironically underlying Wright's suggestions for the building of a new Africa is the fact that he was a Western man, despite his skin color. As such, his frame of reference was Western. He could dismiss or approve what he understood to be African life only in terms of his Western background. When he tells Nkrumah that he is convinced that "the cultural conditioning of the Africans will make it difficult for them to adjust quickly to values that are solely Western," he implies that Africans must begin on their road to the future from a starting point of Western values and ideas.[12] Deviations, he says, must sprout from within the unique elements of African culture—a culture that Wright so briefly discerned during his short visit. Although *Black Power* seems to record faithfully Wright's experiences in the Gold Coast and then to convert them into generalizations about African religion, politics, people, and national purpose, the book is primarily a document in Wright's personal history. As such, it establishes Wright as a man conversant with ideas in many areas of thought, surely more than can be distinguished in his diverse works written earlier in America. More important, it dispels any notions that Wright, as a sensitive, articulate, and intellectual Negro, could somehow step out of the stream of Western indoctrination and culture in which he had been immersed.

Black Power thus endorses one certainty: that Wright was a Western man, perhaps more narrowly an American Negro. If in the opening pages of the book he suspects that as a Negro he might be able to bridge a cultural and historical gap, he soon learns that he could never be an African. In fact, in his early fiction and nonfiction he never had indicated that a back-to-Africa movement could be an acceptable solution for the problems of a black man in a white American world. When, for instance, in short scenes in some of his fiction his Negro characters discuss the palatability of such a movement, they become unresponsive. They place their trust for the future within their American culture and on the white man's soil. In *Lawd Today*, while Jake Jackson and his friends watch a parade sponsored by a back-to-Africa organization, their conversation reflects a faith in an American destiny:

> "You know what I don't like about them folks?" asked Jake.
> "What?"
> "They wants us to go back to Africa."
> "I don't like that, neither."
> "They's sure nuts on that point."
> "And if we went back to Africa, what would we do?"
> "You'll have to ask them that."
> "Aw. . . . They nuts as hell," said Jake, with an impatient wave of the hand.[13]

As with the sparse Marxist material in the novel, the back-to-Africa movement remains unexplored as a resolution for Jake's miserably deprived life and personality. Nowhere in *Lawd Today* does Wright suggest even obliquely that a return to Africa is desirable. Even in *12 Million Black Voices*, Wright's Marxist-tinted poetic-prose history of the American Negro, he reinforces the American foundation upon which his vision for an American-Negro future rests. Rhetorically asking what it is that "black folk" want, he answers, "We want what others have, the right to share in the upward march of American life, the only life we remember or have ever known."[14]

Years after writing *12 Million Black Voices*, Wright set out for the Gold Coast harboring no hidden expectation that Africa could be a haven for the disinherited American Negro or for himself. Yet he was curious whether his color could be the bridge between cultures, whether perhaps he himself was somehow different from a Westerner and in some ways akin to black Africans. Obviously, then, his thinking in this respect had been somewhat modified between 1941 and the early 1950s. On the ship that took him to Africa, after a discussion with African students, he felt that he had shared with them their belief in the primacy of collective action over individual destiny.[15] However, his ramblings through all parts of the Gold Coast, from city movie houses to hinterland tribal huts, severed him from a psychological connection with the African offspring of his African forefathers. He could not sympathize with their inclination to create a present from the past, with no regard for the future.[16] Tribal religions, with their emotionalism and magic, also troubled him; and the worship of ancestors he called "daylight dreams," symbolic of a repulsive African sense of reality.[17]

Wright uncovered other social and cultural differences, all pointing unwaveringly to the truth that he indeed was an alien to the thought and culture of the Gold Coast. A concise statement about the impact of the African trip upon Wright has been made by Harold R. Isaacs, who confirms that it was "the lack of modern thinking that assailed his Western-style intelligence. For Wright reacted . . . as a rationalist who had put his faith in the power of the mind to conquer ignorance and violence." Isaacs continues that Wright "left the country as he had come, full of . . . general bonds of political solidarity and sympathy, but still a stranger." Shaken by what he had learned about the nature of African culture, Wright "never did find it easy to open channels of communication with Africans."[18]

On the ship returning him to Europe, Wright penned his letter to Nkrumah. In it, he clearly states his only personal point of empathetic contiguity with black Africans: "While roaming at random . . . I felt an odd kind of at-homeness, a solidarity that stemmed not from ties of blood or race, or from being of African descent, but from the quality of deep hope and suffering embedded in the lives of your people, from the hard facts of oppression that cut across time, space, and culture."[19] Wright then specifically refers to himself as "an American Negro."

The circumstances surrounding Wright's decision to travel to Indonesia in 1955 were much like those leading to his African visit. Accidentally eyeing a newspaper item announcing a meeting of twenty-nine African and Asian nations to be held in Bandung in the spring of 1955, Wright mused whether he too should attend as an observer. He thought that the range of the planned discussions would be sufficiently broad to stimulate many of his own interests —racialism, colonialism, international economic and social cooperation, and world peace. As a Negro and an ex-Communist Party member, he reasoned that he could understand the immediate concerns of the emergent new nations. Searching for a theme that could somehow connect the backgrounds of the Africans and Asians to be attending the conference, he isolated two elements: "The nations sponsoring the conference . . . were all religious. . . . This smacked of something new, something beyond Left and Right. Looked at in terms of history, these nations repre-sented *races* and *religions*, vague but potent forces."[20]

In his published account of his Bandung trip, *The Color Curtain*, Wright does indeed stress race and religion. Race was a subject he knew well, and in his observations on racial issues affecting the conference, he is both perceptive and articulate. Religion was, however, another matter for Wright. About it he speaks from a great distance. He un-derstood it only as it was a force to be reckoned with. He could not grasp exactly how religious belief could be con-verted into political action and policy, although at the conference he did sense that African-Asian religious beliefs were being carried to the political forum. His reasoning is specious that because he "grew up in the Methodist and Seventh Day Adventist churches and . . . saw and observed religion in . . . childhood," he could, therefore, identify with and explain the religious backgrounds of certain African-Asian political ventures.[21]

Nevertheless, *The Color Curtain* contains much that is revealing about its author and about the political phenomena that he observed. Harold R. Isaacs's comments are valuable and concise for shaping a general assessment of *The Color Curtain*:

Wright is often strident and naïve and stretches some of his points until they snap. . . . But even if he was not Balboa looking out over this turbulent sea, Wright brought special perceptions and emotions to bear upon his discoveries. They took him swiftly, unhindered by too much encumbering knowledge, to the sharp edges of many an Asian-African dilemma.[22]

In addition, Wright is able to discuss communism in Africa and Asia in a relatively unemotional manner, even though he had long since established himself as a firm anti-Communist.

Technically, *The Color Curtain* is not a travel book, but a report (as its subtitle indicates). Yet the first half of the book recounts Wright's journey: Paris to Madrid by train and then from Madrid to Jakarta by plane, with short stops at Cairo, Karachi, Calcutta, and Bangkok. This reconstruction of the trip serves two purposes: it allows Wright and his readers, through interviews on the train and plane, a glimpse of the historical background of the conference; and it contributes a sense of movement from one world toward another, from West to East. Scattered authorial comments about the changing scenery below the airplane parallel the nature of the interviews that Wright engages in on the plane.

The interviewed informants talk about two separate and distinct worlds, while Wright occasionally notes the plane's approach to Jakarta from the West over the diverse landscape below. When Wright is thrust into the teeming brown and yellow masses of Jakarta, no sudden shock ensues; for both he and his audience have been prepared for a world of different sights, sounds, and thought. Brief descriptive passages of Jakarta set the physical stage for the gathering of Africans and Asians at Bandung. Then Wright moves immediately into the business of the conference.

Much of *The Color Curtain*—a shorter volume than *Black Power*—is comprised of excerpts from official speeches and from private interviews, one with the late prime minister of India, Jawaharlal Nehru. The book's weightiest matters loom when Wright discusses Asian communism, world racial affairs, and the future of the nations freed from colonialism. His method of focusing attention on Communist China and on communism itself as an overwhelmingly important force in Asia is commendable. Quickly but convincingly he explains the distrust in Eastern minds of the West, a feeling accumulated over centuries of Western racial and political domination. He then uses information collected in interviews to create a stereotype of a general Eastern mind that is receptive to the idea of collective action rather than individual achievement. The political ramifications are apparent. Speaking of his typical African-Asian man, Wright says: "This propensity for the organically collective . . . propelled him, irrespective of ideology, toward those collectivist visions emanating from Peking and Moscow. . . . And all the fervid adjurations of Washington, London, or Paris to strive for individual glory . . . left him cold and suspicious."[23] Therefore, the tactics of Premier Chou En-lai during the conference acquired a crucial aspect, and Wright asserts that a masterstroke of political deftness was accomplished when

Chou En-lai elected in his major speech to concentrate upon African-Asian unity rather than upon East-West political and ideological conflict. Chou's identification with those millions of Easterners who were seemingly rejected by the West set him and his country, with its own nearly uncountable multitudes, into both a leadership and a showcase position.[24]

What the reactions were among the other representatives is not revealed, though Wright claims that no evident opposition to Chou developed during the conference. Wright does not belittle the attractiveness of Marxism for either the Africans or the Asians. Communism and China have an advantage in both Asia and Africa, since, according to Wright, the West has offered no effective program for the self-vitalization of the new nations. In fact, he claims, the West "is still discussing whether the Africans have the capacity for self-government."[25] Although Wright congratulates the Asian Communists for their political poise and perspicuity, he does admit at the end of *The Color Curtain* his personal Western and anti-Communist sympathies. Thus, his earlier representation of communism as the likely star of destiny for Africa and Asia emerges not as a solution, but as a threat to both West and East.[26]

Although Wright is concerned about the future of the masses in Asia and Africa, the tone of his remarks in *The Color Curtain* implies a disquietude about his own figurative survival and about the endurance of the cultures he had allied himself with, that is, the Western world outside of Russia and countries affiliated with it. Despite his disclosure that a prime force underlying the Eastern present and future is the sense of common racial solidarity apart from the white race, he knows that in a conflict between East and West, Easterners would view the colored peoples in the West as enemies, not friendly kin. Realizing the perilously sensitive state of political affairs between the

Communist nations and the non-Communist Western nations, he wants the new African-Asian nations to pursue their own course to the future, unthreatened by the economic and military forces of the United States, Soviet Russia, or Communist China.[27] Thus, in terms of world peace, a Communist revolution sponsored by Russia or Communist China would be as dangerous as a Western infiltration and domination.

Wright appears to have supported a "third force" to alleviate, through political and ideological complication, the tensions between a Communist East and a non-Communist West, so that the "secular, rational base of thought and feeling in the Western world" might be influential in counteracting the potential fanatical racist and religious basis of action in Africa and Asia.[28] At the same time, he uses the recent Marxist history of Russia and China to stress that the adoption of communism by the new nations would encourage a rigidity permitting no dissenter to cross its path unscathed. He refers to Chou En-lai's regime in China as one of "drastic theories and practices of endless secular sacrifices," and he calls the Stalinist Russian approach one of "limitless murder and terror." If either the Africans or the Asians were to choose communism, they would be following a "bloody path"—but such a course would be preferable to a new Western domination. Wright thinks that the Russian Stalinists were satisfied that they had done what was "brutally necessary" to industrialize quickly and to protect themselves from external, armed threats. He wonders, though, whether this "tragic method, with its secular religiosity of horror and blood," should be repeated.[29]

This negative inference is a reassertion of Wright's vehemently anti-Communist sentiment, an attitude laudably shielded from his readers until the conclusion of *The Color Curtain*. It helps to clarify Wright's earlier recommendations to Nkrumah in the public letter in *Black Power*. Blood baths were obviously repulsive to Wright; so too was a strict dedication to Marxist ideology and the practices fostered by it, although he would not condemn the use of a Marxist interpretation of past colonial history. Wright preferred pragmatic policies, primed by responsible African-Asian leadership, that would channel mass energies away from emotional nationalism toward what he thought was "Western rationalism."[30] The West should accept gracefully a fresh configuration of nations that through African-Asian ownership and development of its own resources would reflect a third industrial and cultural power-force in the world.[31] In other words, in *The Color Curtain*, Wright is advocating a Western withdrawal and a "hands-off" policy. His position analogizes well with that of the American colonists and revolutionists in respect to England. Moreover, it places Wright in a humanistic and political tradition that contends that the essence of human dignity and freedom rests in the promotion of pragmatic self-determination and self-identification, unshackled by ideology and external forces. For Wright, however, twentieth-century industrialization had to be an undeniable ingredient of any African-Asian goals.

Wright's outlook for the future of the colored nations was not without reservations. His overriding fear was that racism would become the edifice around which the African-Asian peoples would construct their framework for world politics and power. His trip to the African Gold Coast bared for him the effects of white racism on Africans, and in *Black Power* he is apprehensive that a combination of irrational religious forces and a militant reaction to white racism will sabotage an orderly and rational embarkation on independence, let alone invite chaos in world affairs. In *The Color Curtain* he conveys similar misgivings. As an American Negro, he well understood how easily a black racist position could be assumed. As a traveler to ex-colonies of the West and as an interviewer of the new colored nationalists, he quickly and acutely sensed that both Africans and Asians might emotionally and vindictively reverse the racist deeds of their white colonial masters. If in Wright's early fiction there is the slightest undercurrent of black racism or nationalism, in *The Color Curtain* Wright emphatically demolishes the possibility that such an attitude lurks behind his artistry or his politically oriented works of the 1950s. Although his protests against white racism, of course, date back to the 1930s, in *The Color Curtain* he deplores *any* sort of racism, calling it "evil" and "loathsome."[32] The signs of a new racism that he saw rising in Africa and Asia told him that if a thermonuclear weapon were to fall on Asian soil from Western aircraft, every white person in sight would be slain by the surviving Asians, so intense were their feelings against the West on racial grounds alone.[33]

Although in *The Color Curtain* Wright is not a prophet of doom, the import of his remarks is to the Western world as distressing as are the messages filtering through the many descriptions in the lengthier *Black Power*. In subject matter and ultimate effect, the two books are companion pieces. Both portray an author who is as sympathetically concerned about the plight, aspirations, and future of the African-Asian nations as he is solicitously restive about the destiny of Western existence. Like *Black Power*, *The Color Curtain* is a confirmation of the Western nature and character of Wright's interests and thoughts. Both also mark his abandonment of ideology as a guide for political action.

Many of the basic concepts that Wright set down in *Black Power* and *The Color Curtain* are concisely repeated, reinforced, and clarified in the essays collected in *White Man, Listen!*, published in late 1957. This work originated from lectures that Wright delivered in European cities between 1950 and 1956.[34] Only one essay, "The Literature of the Negro in the United States," was written before Wright's ventures into Africa and Asia. The other three— "The Psychological Reactions of Oppressed Peoples," "Tradition and Industrialization," and "The Miracle of Nationalism in the African Gold Coast"—were composed after the journeys. Because the four essays were derived from lectures and thus were probably written with the presence of a live audience in mind, they are in many places personal, sometimes almost chatty. At other points the words are charged with a distinct weightiness, tending in fact toward pontification. Wright does not allow his audience to evade for long the seriousness of the matters he had elected to discuss.

Despite a majority of remarks directed toward international race relations and politics, an absorbing feature of *White Man, Listen!* is Wright's preoccupation with discovering a definition of himself in terms of a regional outlook, either Western or African-Asian. What he had already established about himself, although unconsciously so, in *Black Power* and *The Color Curtain* he now at last is examining and deliberating upon. It is as though he were finally joining his audience in viewing the personally significant elements that had issued unrecognized by him from the two earlier politically oriented volumes. Although his self-observations are at times contradictory and reflect a certain confusion, they do touch the essence of his approach to many problems and situations during his post-American years: they underscore his Western-inspired rationalist premises.

Although the introductory section asserts that Wright has no need for "as many emotional attachments, sustaining roots, or idealistic allegiances as most people," and that he likes, and even cherishes, what he calls his "state of abandonment, of aloneness," the remainder of *White Man,*

Listen! is further testimony to the Western rational foundation that helped to form his perspectives.[35] He came to realize that his position as a Negro in Western culture tended to create a dichotomy; for, on the one hand, he was a product of Western civilization and thought, whereas, on the other, he was a man with a racial identity, who had never been permitted "to blend, in a natural and healthy manner, with the culture and civilization of the West." His being black in the West resulted in "a psychological distance" between Wright and his Western environment. However, this interval was not a void: in it resided a chronically skeptical and critical temperament, itself a vital ingredient or catalyst of Western philosophy. Consequently, as Wright showed signs of recognizing, his impulses to step out of the stream of Western thought were borne perhaps as much by a characteristically Western indoctrination as by his alienation from his white-dominated environment. Having rejected an Eastern outlook because he thought that it was controlled by religious and emotional attitudes, he makes in *White Man, Listen!* the questionable assertion that he can presently see "both worlds from another and third point of view."[36] Perhaps Wright means that his vision is not cluttered by those elements of Western thought which also contain something of the irrational and the emotional— points emphasized when in *White Man, Listen!* he discusses historical Western policies and dispositions toward their colored colonial subjects. Nevertheless, when he suggests to African and Asian leaders the possible courses of action open to them in their new independent nations, he implores them to be guided by the spirit of the European Enlightenment and the Reformation.[37]

White Man, Listen! is dedicated to "the Westernized and tragic elite of Asia, Africa, and the West Indies— . . . men who carry on their frail but indefatigable shoulders the best of two worlds."[38] It is to them (and to Western leaders) that Wright directs his observations and comments in the section entitled "Tradition and Industrialization." Stressing that the key to his Western modernity is his secular outlook, Wright cautions African-Asian leaders that before they can advance their people into the twentieth century, they must sweep away emotional and religious rationalizations. They should, in fact, adopt his view that "sheer brute man" has a value outside of mystical forces and can nourish and find meaning in human life through "a tough-souled pragmatism, implemented by trial and error."[39] In essence, Wright is asking leaders such as Nehru, Sukarno, Nasser, and Nkrumah—all educated in Western ideals and traditions and, he hopes, all sustained by a drive toward establishing orderly institutions in their own countries—to stem the tide of racism and religious fanaticism in the African-Asian world. At the same time, these leaders are implored never to lose sight of a larger goal—political and personal freedom for those whom they might arbitrarily rule for a while. An indispensable first step, of course, is to "become industrialized and powerful, . . . like the West."[40]

However, for its own eventual security and benefit, the West itself has an obligation to discourage African-Asian policies based on fanatical racism and religion by allaying African-Asian fears that new Western interferences would be forthcoming. In a bold and loud voice Wright outlines that responsibility: "THE WEST . . . MUST BE PREPARED TO ACCORD TO THE ELITE OF ASIA AND AFRICA A FREEDOM WHICH IT ITSELF NEVER PERMITTED IN ITS OWN DOMAIN. THE ASIAN AND AFRICAN ELITE MUST BE GIVEN ITS HEAD!" Wright's preference for a Western policy of noninterference is clearly reiterated, even in the face of the quasi-dictatorial methods Westerners must nervously watch being imposed by African-Asian leaders. His optimistic explanation here is that the Western-educated leaders will surrender their powers to the people as soon as their practices have established order.[41]

As in *Black Power* and *The Color Curtain*, Wright seems to overrationalize, to express naïveté rather than realistic political sense. Also, as in the two earlier works, Wright displays an acumen sensitive to certain motivations within the colored African-Asian masses that are repulsive to him. However, these perceptions are accompanied by his strong faith in man's unfettered will to accomplish good and justice—a characteristically Western humanistic idea. In the political sections in *White Man, Listen!* as in *Black Power* and *The Color Curtain*, there is thus a strange amalgam of a skepticism and a hopeful optimism.

The background for Wright's political comments is sketched in the opening chapter, "The Psychological Reactions of Oppressed Peoples." In it he makes no attempt to interpret Western influence on, and domination of, African and Eastern countries in the terms of Marxist definitions. Wright, in the 1950s, was willing to admit openly that a "racial structure of life and history itself" exists beyond the patterns of class history.[42] The rest of this chapter merely synthesizes Wright's thinking in *Black Power* and *The Color Curtain* about the composite personalities of the ex-colonial nationalists. He examines their psychological shortcomings —often the result of subjugation by the West—and tries to forecast the possible future directions for both their emotions and their reason. He concludes by indicating that "the historical hour is late" and that the white man should guard against a reaction to emergent colored peoples that could result in a tragic and foolish unleashing of thermonuclear weapons upon the East.[43]

The section on Negro literature in the United States initially appears to be a digression from the political and sociological materials in *White Man, Listen!* However, it is in a way an integrated piece, for its theme has a bearing on the other chapters. Wright traces the content of American-Negro poetry from Phillis Wheatley, who wrote in the late eighteenth century, to himself in the 1930s. In effect, he outlines a gradual shift in American-Negro poetry from universal themes to racial protest. Linking this transformation to the gradual estrangement of the American Negro from the larger American culture, Wright then explains why Marxist attitudes seem to have permeated much Negro poetry after World War I. Simply, the Negro had temporarily found an ideology with which to order his frustrated American experience.[44] Wright halts his commentary short of the post-World War II period, but notes that in the novels of Ralph Ellison, James Baldwin, Chester Himes, Frank Yerby, and other Negro writers there is "a sharp loss of lyricism, a drastic reduction of the racial content, a rise in preoccupation with urban themes and subject matter."[45]

Having begun the essay by declaring that such non-American Negroes as Alexander Pushkin and Alexandre Dumas were able to concentrate their artistic efforts on universal themes because they had been accepted in and integrated with their respective societies and cultures, he points to the post-World War II developments in Negro writing as an important sign for both Negroes and whites in America. They mark the inception of a return to the spirit of the time when Phillis Wheatley felt at home in her environment, when she "was at one with her culture."[46] Wright's concluding passage may be extrapolated beyond the narrow limits of American letters:

If . . . our Negro expression broadens, assumes the common themes and burdens of literary expression which are the heritage of all men, then by that token you will know that a humane attitude prevails in America towards us. And a gain in humaneness in America is a gain in humaneness for us all. When that day comes, there will exist one more proof of the oneness of man, of the basic unity of human life on this earth.[47]

There is an evident connection between this statement and Wright's vision for a peaceful and rational world of all nations and all colors. A rapidly integrated America becomes the symbol for a world that will structure its policies and organizations around a concept of man as man, not man as the embodiment of race, social class, or ideology. Although the section on American-Negro literature seems to be a digressive but informative and delightful portion of *White Man, Listen!* it is, in fact, consistent with the thematic framework of the book.

Pagan Spain (1957) approximates more nearly than *Black Power* and *The Color Curtain* the popular idea of what travel literature should be. It contains numerous descriptive scenes of countrysides, cities, churches, public buildings, grottoes, and the like. However, as the adjective in the title implies, the book is intended to be more than a depiction of the physical characteristics of Spain. It is a bid at defining the heart and the soul of the Spanish people, individually and collectively, and of the nation generally; the title concisely tells us what Wright discovered Spain to be. Because Wright had more time in Spain than he had in either the Gold Coast or Indonesia, he was able to move at a leisurely pace as he gathered information, conducted interviews, attended public events, and digested all that he had seen, heard, and experienced. He recorded these episodes and encounters with the people, along with sufficient portrayals of the scenery around him, to give a sense of real locale to his immediate, intellectual, and emotional responses and impressions.

Wright's Spanish trip was inspired by a sudden impulse, in much the same way as had been his journey to Africa and as would be his subsequent one to Indonesia. Driving his car beneath the clear blue canopy of a southern French sky during a torrid day in August 1954, Wright suddenly resolved to turn toward Spain, a country many of his friends had been urging him to visit. At the time he was a man with "no commitments" to work or pleasure. However, he could hardly have envisioned that his expedition would last until mid-December and would be continued in the late spring of the following year.[48] His journeys would carry him to all the large and famous cities of Spain—Barcelona, Madrid, Seville, Guadalajara, Toledo—even to Gibraltar and across the Mediterranean for a brief stop in Tangier. Furthermore, there would be visits to rural villages, country shrines, urban churches, barrooms, bullfights, and gypsy quarters; and there would be interviews with flamenco dancers, clerks, prostitutes, intellectuals, aristocrats, bullfighters, government officials—in short, with a wide sampling of the Spanish people.[49]

Wright's account of his visit begins with a focus on politics. It ends with an immersion in socio-religious criticism. *Pagan Spain*, in fact, is a scathing attack on the Roman Catholic church in Spain. Wright's understanding of Spain comes from a study of religious and psychological forces, not political affairs and institutions. From the opening page to the last, he never alters his belief that Franco has headed an absolutist regime and that the outcome of the Spanish civil war marked the death of hope for Spanish freedom. However, as Wright became more deeply engaged in the private and public lives of the Spaniards, he began to comprehend that behind the politics, the civil unrest, and the contradictions in Spanish life resides the most decisive factor—religion.

Pagan Spain is a mixture of strange ingredients—political analysis, sexual study, and interpretations centered around religion. It also contains the traveler's keen probings beneath the surface appearances of a nation to its well-disguised realities. On one level, *Pagan Spain* is a review of practice, policy, custom, and habit of a nation. On another level, it gradually penetrates downward to the psychology of a people. Behind all is the traveler-writer, digging, asking, seeking, experiencing, and meditating. Sensual visual perception is combined with thoughtful personal insight. Although few of the Catholic church's dogmas and precepts are examined by Wright, his selection of church-related scenes, interviews, and writings is so skillfully and vividly handled that his conclusions are persuasive. If there is an immediately detectable weakness, it is Wright's tendency to generalize about the whole of a people, even when certain interviews have introduced the exceptions. One result of this tendency is a questioning about the degree to which the generalizations may apply.

To maintain a focus on the broad theme of appearance and reality—figuratively on the contrast between a fictional Spain and a true Spain—Wright employs a simple but clever device. Early in his visit he had acquired a copy of *Formación Política: Lecciones para las Flechas* (*"Political Formation: Lessons for the Arrows"*). A handbook treating the aims and principles of the Franco regime, it was to be studied by young aspirants to positions of service in the government. It consisted of questions about Spain's history, Franco's Falange Party, and the relationship of the Catholic church to the government and the people; and it provided short, simple, and propagandistic answers. By inserting passages from the handbook at convenient intervals in *Pagan Spain*, Wright is able to contrast the Spain he saw, heard, and felt with the Spain portrayed by the Falange. The result is devastating to the Falangists' picture of their country. If one of Wright's intentions at the beginning of his journey was to confirm the dictatorial nature of Franco's rule, the militant handbook offered him a potent weapon. In a single deft move, Wright turned this propagandistic piece upon its maker, while effectively using it as a part of the structure of his work. However, he became increasingly fascinated with the handbook's religious content. As his concentration in *Pagan Spain* shifts from narrower political concerns to broader religious ones, he selects those passages which pertain to church indoctrination rather than to political indoctrination. In effect, Wright's case for exposing a Fascist regime is established early and then is buried, as the more challenging question of the church's role in Spanish life emerges. In either area, however, the insertion of the handbook material is both striking and clever.

Wright's approach to the subject of the Spanish church is accompanied by his growing awareness of the psychological motives behind the actions and the words of the Spaniards he met. As his personal contacts widened, his vision narrowed to a common denominator binding the people—their attitude toward sex. As he examined this particular feature of Spanish life, he inevitably discovered the church to be the perpetrator, if not the force, behind the attitude. His reasoning seems logical. Noting the contradiction between open prostitution and the almost-fanatically high regard Spanish men hold for a virtuous woman, Wright links this paradox to the church's outlook that prostitution is a proof of sin and an indication that the work of salvation has not been completed. Thus, the Spanish people can approve of the ideal. At the same time, their need to witness sin before their own eyes, in order to possess a contrast with the ideal, amounts to a condonation of the existence of the sinful.[50] Probing deeper into the psychology of such a position, he detects that because of the church the Spanish personality is composed of a seething undercurrent of inhibited impulses and thwarted instincts.[51] Relief may be gained through "sinning," which in itself creates a greater sense of guilt. However the exterior of

Spanish life provides outlets of its own in the form of religious processions and festivals and of bullfighting. Through these devices a disturbed psychology may be released in religiously and socially acceptable ways, although Wright feels that such devious manifestations themselves were signs of a greater social sickness.

Wright describes two very different scenes to emphasize the relationship between Spanish cultural and religious practices and sexual attitudes. At the shrine of the Black Virgin of Monserrat, he notes that the religious fervor of the Spanish visitors carried with it an undertone of the sensuous. After some private deliberations, he declares that the Black Virgin represents one way Spanish Catholics can accept without guilt the more instinctive feelings about sex—which Wright claims is "the most prevalent, powerful, emotional, and factual experience in human life." A worshiping of the Black Virgin really then adumbrates an idolization of the female principle of life, itself bound up in a physical, sexual vision.[52] Responsible for an unnatural channeling of natural forces, the church itself has transgressed against, and warped, the personalities of a people. Wright depicts many other scenes in which the church is the culprit behind the misguided and emotionally exploited Spaniards. In a final portrait—of a procession at a spring religious festival in Seville—he culminates his gradual erection of a pagan frame around Spanish Catholicism. The procession serves to reinforce Wright's earlier statement that "*Spain was not yet even Christian!*" Instead, the pagan streams of influence, nurtured by the church, had left Spain behind Western thought somewhere near the Dark Ages, even outside of modern Catholicism, with the older paganism intact.[53]

The religious settings and activities described in *Pagan Spain* point to a contorted Spanish psychology. So do selected secular events, which are, Wright argues, outgrowths of the church's influences. In one of the best-written and most descriptive portions of the book, Wright uses the bull-fights to illustrate his contention.[54] The matador is compared to a high priest who offers the symbol of a sacrifice to the crowd; the bull becomes an expansion of man's dark instincts. There can be no doubt that the beast must be killed. His death *"must serve as a secular baptism of emotion to wash the heart clean of its illegal dirt."*[55] It seems clear to Wright that the "illegal dirt" is sex, especially after he has beheld in astonishment a crowd's impulsive and animalistic reaction to the killing of a bull in a makeshift, rural bullring. At the end of the slaughter, the spectators wildly surged toward the dead bull, then kicked, stomped on, and ground out the bull's testicles, pouring out "the hate and frustration and bewilderment of their troubled and confused consciousnesses."[56]

Much of Spanish life, in Wright's view, is a result of such distortions in psyches caused by the church. Contradictory attitudes toward sex—the worshiping of it in a symbolic church event and the metaphorical crushing of it in a secular rite—are merely pieces in a larger puzzle that will expose the church as the evil and selfish villain creating the picture. A willing and devilish ally, to be sure, is the fascistic Falange; but even it is the product of a larger whole. The summary of Wright's profile of Spain is simple enough: "the prostitution, the corruption, the economics, the politics had about them a sacred aura. *All was religion in Spain.*"[57]

As for the Spanish civil war, the historical event that had influenced Wright's preconceptions about the country, it too occupies a small though significant place within a larger concept. A journalist friend supplied Wright with the proper words: "we butchered one another and loved it." The war is further proof, as the anonymous journalist states, that Spaniards are "barbarians"; only those who know that Spaniards *are* barbarians "are a bit civilized."[58] Completing Wright's logic, one may assume that the barbarity of Spain is an offspring of its paganism, which itself is a condition of a mind born of and fed by Spanish Catholicism.

The accuracy of Wright's view of a nation is, of course, open to question. *Pagan Spain* does, however, tell us much about its author. The journey through Spain was for Wright an educational experience, but only in terms of a limited land area, a specific culture, and a fraction of the world's population. Although a Western country, Spain has rarely been in the stream of Western thought and culture that Wright had associated with Protestantism. His visit to Africa had been a contact with foreign, non-Western regions of the world. In a sense, so was his trip to Spain. The irrational aspects of African culture and, later, of Asian culture had repulsed him. So did similar aspects of Spanish culture.

Black Power, *The Color Curtain*, and *White Man, Listen!* all attest to the fact that Wright embarked on his journeys to other lands with certain biases. In *Pagan Spain* he says that he tried to sweep from his mind his "inescapable Protestant background and conditioning, . . . irredeemably secular attitude, and . . . temperamental inability to accept childlike explanations of a universe."[59] However, his reactions to Spain seem to have been dominated by these underlying foundations of thought. When he asserts that the real difference between Spain and other Western countries "lay in the area of the secular that Western man . . . had won and wrung from his own religious and irrational consciousness," he really underlines his own position or bias while proffering what he feels is an objective view of Spain.[60] Even if Wright's image of Spain should approach a valid and objective reproduction, his predispositions cannot be overlooked. In *Pagan Spain*, as in his other nonfictional works resulting from his travels during the 1950s, there is that consistent framework of thought which had helped to influence his embracement in the 1930s of the seemingly rational, pseudo-scientific, secular tenets of Marxism. Perhaps, too, from a related conviction that man's rational mind could and should be the source for the resolution of Negro-white problems, Wright sounds his protest, trusting that his voice will be heard and heeded by other rational men. Although such works as *Black Power, The Color Curtain, White Man, Listen!* and *Pagan Spain* indicate new and wider concerns on the part of Wright, the messages found in each identify and establish a basis from which these concerns stemmed— Wright's desire for an orderly and rational universe, created by man out of the concept of his own rational and humane image.

CHAPTER 4

The Philosophical
Premises

WRIGHT'S NONFICTION of the 1950s, published in the decade before his sudden death in 1960, strongly suggests the presence of an underlying, vaguely articulated, perhaps personally unidentified, broad base of humanistic thought akin to eighteenth-century European rational idealism. Yet, throughout his literary career, Wright indulged much of his mental and artistic energies in the exploration of concepts related to the philosophies and studies of nineteenth- and twentieth-century figures such as Nietzsche, Kierkegaard, Husserl, Heidegger, Jaspers, Camus, Sartre —all associated with existentialism—and Freud, in addition to Hegel, Marx, Engels, and Lenin.[1] However, the philosophical premises from which Wright operated do not ostensibly form a neat and consistent pattern. Although the influence of Marxism on him implies a view that perceives man and society engaged in progress, the impact of the existentialists could have evoked a vision skeptical about human and social progress, bringing out the absurdity of such a concept and even of life itself.[2] In addition, the spirit of humanistic rationalism permeating Wright's late nonfiction often seems to be a qualified one.

It is tempered by his personal history of investigation into the psychology and philosophy of the irrational—although investigation does not necessarily mean complete acceptance. Also, Wright surely had always to contend with the inner pessimism and bitterness that must have accompanied his recognition of the state of race relations in America.

Near the end of his life, Wright appears to have been defining the concept of "rational mind" in terms of what he felt was a human capability for placing into some sort of rational structure those elements of the mind and of society which are ostensibly irrational. In effect, he seemed to be shaping a belief that from chaos could come order. He reasoned that chaos was man-made, and hence its psychic and social sources could be discovered, analyzed, understood, and, hopefully, either eliminated or altered to conform to an ideal, orderly, human universe in which every man could find security, personal meaning, and individual dignity. Even Wright's protest literature, although it bares a wrathful author, was intended to change the world and to improve the lot of all men, that is, to foster progress. Marxism gave Wright an economic and social formula in the 1930s and the early 1940s. With his later disenchantment with the Communist Party (but not necessarily with certain Marxist ideals), antiprogressive notes in his thinking and learning began to intrude more and more into his writing. Man's alienation from man is a theme that grows stronger from *Native Son* (1940) to his long short-story "The Man Who Lived Underground" (1944). In 1953 the theme had apparently completely taken over the content of *The Outsider*; but, as we shall see later in this chapter, that novel in fact rejects the very existential precepts that the book's main character lives by. When *The Outsider* is considered together with Wright's nonfiction of the 1950s, it reinforces our sense of an authorial disposition valuing contact and cooperation among people to produce improved personal psychic conditions and social configurations.

Because of his tragic experiences as an American Negro, Wright could easily have retreated into a state of despair and pessimism, but the positive aspects of his works—the hopes for the future and for progress—overshadow the negative ones. His outraged cries against social injustices, his almost-compulsive drive to create scenes of violence and destruction in his fiction, his overwhelming concentration on the mental anguishes of his characters, his portrayals of psychic and social worlds in which irrational ideas and deeds often prevail—all are not convincing enough to dissolve the rational idealist behind them. Stated differently, Wright often lived out in his works two principal facets of his own psyche: one part was composed of his immediate reflexive reactions to a world potentially bent upon devouring him. The other part consisted of a self-image of the moral and intellectual man, intently working toward transforming a threatening and chaotic world into a secure and just earthly paradise for everybody. This second side revealed itself clearly in his nonfiction of the 1950s. Actually, it had been reflected earlier in his belief in Marxist ideals, even after his disillusionment with the Communist Party. Wright continually tried to fulfill himself as a moral agent. Although he often shocked his readers by depicting terror, violence, irrationality, and human alienation, his desire was that this shock treatment would help in breaking down prejudice and ignorance and in creating a rational world—a world, for him in particular, in which a Negro would be a man, not a Negro. As *Black Boy* so powerfully tells us, Wright's own search for this goal was initiated in his youth. It seems to have coursed a circular route—from questions demanding rational answers, to axiomatic answers based on pseudo-rational thought (Marxism in the form of the Communist Party), to a belief that rational truth and rational order could be attained despite the existence of irrational thought and deed.

It is difficult—in most cases impossible—and not entirely fair to reconstruct exactly how an author has applied to his own work the knowledge and thinking acquired from others. With Wright we know at least that into certain works he incorporated ideas of noted European intellectuals, although not in simple eclectic fashion. Variations, amalgamations, and even refutations occurred. Wright often provided a clue to his sources through epigraphs attached to both his fiction and nonfiction and through direct references in his nonfiction, but not one of his works systematically follows materials borrowed from other thinkers. Whether he misunderstood or misinterpreted such men as Freud, Nietzsche, and Kierkegaard is another matter and is hard to distinguish from intentional modulations, combinations, or refutations. Nevertheless, despite his partial reliance on ideas proferred by others, he remained faithful, after his period of involvement with the Communist Party, to his own desires and abilities to create a personal vision of life.

One early influence was certain works by Henry Louis Mencken, whose interest in Nietzsche apparently inspired Wright to read Nietzsche.[3] Works such as *Native Son*, *The Outsider*, *Savage Holiday*, and "The Man Who Lived Underground" may be studied generally within the terms of Nietzscheism, in addition to existentialism and Freudianism. Wright's works before World War II often depend on Marxism for a favorable frame of reference; but they also reflect opposition to formal religion, specifically to formal Christianity, as a solution to problems primarily secular. *Native Son*, with its elements of Marxist propaganda, contains an unconscious existentialism, which is evident to a greater degree in "The Man Who Lived Underground," itself influenced by Wright's admitted interest in Dostoyevsky. In *The Outsider* and his nonfiction of the 1950s, Wright obviously and consciously used, in one way or another, precepts formulated by the existentialists, among them his friend in Paris, Jean-Paul Sartre. However, before his philosophical journeys from Nietzsche to Sartre, he must have been influenced by ideas more easily accessible in his everyday life.

Wright's initial associations with metaphysical thought were in his Christian religious indoctrination. However, as a Negro in a poverty-stricken and generally uneducated class of Southern society, he must have had little or no contact with the sophisticated theological and philosophical aspects of the Baptist and the Methodist forms of Protestantism that he was exposed to in his home and in rural and small-town environments. *Black Boy* reinforces this speculation. Wright vividly describes the proddings of his mother and grandmother for him to acquire an unshaking faith in their Protestant religion. He also pictures scenes of church hymn-singing and of congregation members wildly screaming and gesturing in their contacts with invisible spirits. (Although not so intensely depicted, these scenes in *Black Boy* are similar to ones found in James Baldwin's novel of Harlem life, *Go Tell It on the Mountain*.) Wright finally escaped unaffected by religious claims on his emotions, though not without admitting that before his teens he had been attracted to his family's religion:

Many of the religious symbols appealed to my sensibilities and I responded to the dramatic vision of life held by the church, feeling that to live day to day with death as one's sole thought was to be so compassionately sensitive toward life as to view all men as slowly dying, and the trembling sense of fate that welled up, sweet and melancholy, from the hymns blended with the sense of fate that I had already caught from life.[4]

Wright stresses "the sense of fate . . . caught from life" and the gloomier aspects of Protestantism, suffering and death. Like so much in *Black Boy*, this emphasis reflects attitudes deriving from the edges of starvation and privation that the young Wright had approached so often and of an ever-present threat of annihilation at the hands of the foreboding white world.

Commenting about Sunday school at his church, he affirms that "God or His ways" were not to be learned there, but in street life, where there was little joy to suggest the happiness of salvation.[5] At the same time, though, as a teen-ager forced to labor to provide the subsistence of a family without a father and to uphold the little dignity a Negro could have in Jackson, Mississippi, Wright could sense in an ambiguous way that "the bright sunshine and . . . the throbbing life of the people in the streets" somehow served testimony to a belief that the gospel of his church did not possess the keys to explaining the world around him or to providing man with a happiness on earth. The pulpit stories he had heard of "vast lakes of eternal fire, . . . the sun burning to ashes, . . . voices speaking out of clouds, . . . the dead rising and living . . . ," all were unrelated to the agony of his home life and the fears and loneliness of his blackness.[6]

In effect, in his youth Wright was already skeptical about the irrational forces of religion. They seemed to offer no answers for the unordered, seemingly irrational facts of his indigent, Negro existence. At the age of twelve he had, he says, "a predilection for what was real that no argument could ever gainsay" and "a conviction that the meaning of living came only when one was struggling to wring a meaning out of meaningless suffering."[7] A connection between misery here and a promised happiness hereafter was incomprehensible. Obviously, then, Wright's attentions, even in his youth, were directed earthward, toward the state of man as man, not toward man as the potential inheritor of heaven. Factors of social and economic import in his milieu were beginning to capture the center of his life. He could not be content with the solace of a spiritual union with God, when around him he saw men of different races in need of a real union with one another in order to face and resolve the hardships of their social environment.

The problem of whether to allow a place for formal religion in his life inevitably led Wright to ask himself about the existence of a God. His conclusions came sometime soon after the age of twelve. What he decided then, as confessed in *Black Boy*, may be securely accepted as the controlling guidepost for any of his later discussions about his relationship to a God:

His existence or nonexistence never worried me. I reasoned that if there did exist an all-wise, all-powerful God who knew the beginning and the end, who meted out justice to all, who controlled the destiny of man, this God would surely know that I doubted His existence and He would laugh at my foolish denial of Him. And if there was no God at all, then why all the commotion? I could not imagine God pausing in His guidance of unimaginably vast worlds to bother with me.

. . . Before I had been made to go to church, I had given God's existence a sort of tacit assent, but after having seen His creatures serve Him at first hand, I had had my doubts. My faith . . . was welded to the common realities of life, anchored in the sensations of my body and in what my mind could grasp, and nothing could ever shake this faith, and surely not my fear of an invisible power.[8]

To read into this statement the beliefs of Nietzsche or Sartre is indeed tempting, but it would be fallacious. If

Wright in the mid-1940s was accurately reproducing his thinking as a teen-ager in the early 1920s, then no prior system of abstract or practical philosophy may be imposed upon that thinking. Its similarities to philosophies that negate or destroy the existence of a God or can function without a God are accidental; for there is no evidence that Wright, as a boy in the South, was aware of those historical thinkers who later would attract him. However, once we accept the picture of a man who in essence had rejected the theological concepts of Christianity and who had begun to sense the tragic and lonely implications of his experiences as a Negro in a predominantly white society, then we should not be surprised at his subsequent gravitation toward the philosophical literature of the alienated and self-determining man. Even his lengthy pause at the dialectical haven of Hegel and Marx fits a consistent pattern; for although Marxism assumes that men can eventually communicate and live peacefully and happily with other men, once the prescribed social structure has been established, it posits an initial supposition that there is no God and that men can shape a collective destiny. It is not a credit for Marxism that Wright in his youth arrived at a similar position; nor is his early perception that man is entombed in a state of alienation a proof for an existential faith. Important and tangible is the fact that Wright had established for himself an agnostic position and had dismissed Christianity as a pillar for any further metaphysical explorations.

The literature of Wright's Marxist period is not persistently and patently anti-Christian. It is better understood as being centered on race relations and a revolutionary Marxist future. More precisely, his writing during this period is not encumbered by ranting justifications for an antireligious creed. His arguments for Marxism, whether voiced openly or suggested subtly, are not only usually made in reaction to social and economic conditions, but are reinforced by sad portraits from Negro life. Although portions of *Native Son* do represent exceptions, that novel does not acquire its philosophical undertone merely from Bigger Thomas's rejection of Christianity. Only into works written after 1941 does Wright infuse continuously strong and evidently antireligious materials. Sometimes, as in *The Outsider*, they augment and clarify the existential beliefs of a character. Sometimes, particularly in his nonfiction, they underline Wright's disdain for certain irrational motives behind international politics. Generally, Wright's agnostic attitude was overshadowed by other concerns in his publications of the 1930s and early 1940s. Later, it formed an integral part of the content of his fiction and nonfiction. As he moved over the years from a posture of protest against the immediate social environment to one of questing for a meaning in the life of man, he increasingly stated and affirmed the secular, man-centered nature of his search.

Except for significant scenes in *Native Son*, references to religion and a God in Wright's earlier works are sparse. When they are included, they serve a greater goal—the construction of a Marxist world in which the Negro could participate. Wright's picture-prose history of the American Negro, *12 Million Black Voices*, assigns Christianity an important role in Negro life, but even here the stress is on a Marxist interpretation and a secular revolutionary future. Christianity, Wright claims here, was historically the only door to Western culture opened to blacks by the white man. "The Lords of the Land" used it to stem revolt and to appease their own consciences, guilt-ridden by their sensing the contradiction of the existence of slavery in a world of free men. At the same time, a dual attitude on the part of whites, "compounded of a love of gold and

God," fostered a paternalistic code that offered rewards for the Negro's acceptance of Christianity.[9] In the twentieth century, Wright continues, after the mass Negro flight to the Northern industrial cities, Christianity and churchgoing in the North were an unfortunate residuum from Southern Negro rural ways. They were really an opiate, in Marxist terms, to alleviate the despair over the Negro's recognition of blighted urban conditions—conditions that should have inspired revolt rather than refuge in the white man's religious trickery.

Wright's tone is often subdued and subtle, but his mockery of the Negro's participation in formal Christianity is clear. He does show a glimmer of admiration for the women who flocked to city churches and who tried to rebuild the shattered lives of their men and children through prayer; however, he cannot overlook the narrow existence these women were forced to lead within their Black Belts. As for the men and the children, they had already discovered the meaninglessness of their black lives. They wandered through city jungles, distrustful of rewards confined only to heavenly regions. Gradually faint sounds foretelling the future "tumult of battle" would issue from these black men, hinting of the impending struggle of the proletariat against the capitalists that Wright would have liked, at least near the end of the depression and before World War II.[10]

Lawd Today is a fictional rendering of many of the scenes that Wright later conveyed through words and photographs in *12 Million Black Voices*. Jake Jackson's wife, weakened by illness, is a passive viewer of the festering psychological wounds inflicted upon her neighbors in Chicago's Black Belt. She finds only a weak hope and a sad satisfaction in the religious magazines and newspapers she reads. Jake resents her other-worldliness and her earthly physical suffering, which she chooses not to relieve either through sex at home or through the artificial excitements of the underworld and night life of the Black Belt. Though Jake and his friends are nonparticipants in church affairs and services, they do remain constant in their belief in a God, unlike their male counterparts in *12 Million Black Voices*. Wright never bluntly attacks their metaphysical premises. Instead, he presents religion as merely one of many elements in the American Dream inculcated into the fiber of Negro life through the white man's indoctrination. When Jake and his friends discuss the existence of a God, they are made to reveal their unexamined acceptance of a higher controlling Being:

"Funny how some fools can stand up and say there ain't no Gawd."

"Ain't it though?"

"They ought to know somebody *must*'ve started all this."

"It couldn't start by it*self*."

"Nobody but a *fool* couldn't see that."[11]

The irony that Wright intends in this conversation matches that in a few passages concerned with the men's ignorant views on the Communist Party. It is also related to the Marxist idea that man's environment is his own creation and can be altered through united and determined efforts on the part of man, with no assistance from a divine source. Wright elsewhere in *Lawd Today* employs irony to suggest that the path out of the Black Belt for Jake and his cronies should start in a proletarian vision. He uses similar methods to accentuate his belief that the deprivation of urban Negro life is man-made. Theological matters are unimportant; social justice rather than heavenly salvation should be man's public concern. Though Wright's position is obviously antireligious and secular, it never gracelessly intrudes to interfere with his purpose—to picture the realities of life in the Black Belt against the hollow promises of the capitalistic American Dream.

Wright's short stories of the 1930s for the most part deal with Negro-white relationships. Marxism seeps in here and there. One curious exception is "Superstition," published in 1931.[12] Its frame device features a narrator, a Negro businessman, who is telling his houseguests in Chicago the details of strange events that he had witnessed during a recent business trip to a small Southern town. In stilted and formal prose the tale slowly exposes the superstitious belief among members of a Negro family that a death will occur should the entire family gather for a reunion. The narrator had remained in the town long enough to observe the growing apprehension of the elderly parents as one offspring after another unexpectedly arrived at the house for a Christmas celebration. When at last the remaining two sons entered, the mother fell to the floor, fatally stricken with a heart attack caused by a combination of excitement, fear, and superstition.

"Superstition" is a treatment of only an isolated segment of human psychology. Its dramatic tension and resolution depend heavily upon external plot. The Christmas setting does suggest a connection between religion and the irrational, illogical preoccupation of the family. Not a frontal assault on religion, the story does, however, tend to synthesize the irrational elements shaping lives—including Christianity—that the narrator feels display "worthlessness and nothingness" within their "very bleakness."[13] Although a long distance in time and experience from Wright's nonfiction of the 1950s, "Superstition" seems to have been created out of rational and empirical premises similar to those behind his later works. In its own indirect fashion, the tale is also tacitly antireligious, but it intimates no formula for earthly salvation, as do *Lawd Today* and Wright's other stories of the 1930s.

Wright's concentration on Southern racial strife in *Uncle Tom's Children* is increasingly saturated with Marxist materials, so that the final piece in the expanded edition, "Bright and Morning Star," approaches sheer propaganda, despite its praiseworthy aesthetic qualities. Beyond the social and economic concerns of their Marxist content, the stories point to no positive philosophy or metaphysic inspiring the author. Except in "Fire and Cloud," where a preacher is the main character, and in "Bright and Morning Star," where Johnny-Boy's mother at first displays an articulated but dubious faith in the redemptive powers of Christ, Wright does not indulge in argumentation against the values of religion or Christianity. Rather, he causes some characters to transfer their religious zeal from spiritual considerations to social concerns. He does not ask his Southern Negro figures to deny their religion; instead, he pleads with them to place their hope for a better life in social action, not in prayer.

In "Fire and Cloud" a thread of hypocrisy in Southern Christianity is uncovered when Preacher Taylor, after being beaten by white vigilantes, realizes that the town's white minister will offer no assistance, though they both preach the same gospel. However, in the end, the Negroes' religious organization becomes the springboard for social action. Through their church the Negroes can meet together to plan a march and demonstration against the cruel practices of the white-controlled city hall. However, before the church members can reach an accord, Preacher Taylor himself must undergo a transformation. He must separate his religious goals as a preacher from his social obligations as a man, so that to him "the peoples gotta be real as Gawd."[14] Once he has done this, he, as spiritual father of his flock, can lead them in their march, hand in hand with the poor whites of the area. In effect, Wright is condemning Negro Christianity on spiritual grounds less than he is on social grounds. Thus his personal prejudice against the authenticity of theology and religion is not intrusive.

In "Bright and Morning Star," Sue must be won over to the social faith of her Communist son, Johnny-Boy. Her choice is to be one not of displacement, but of separation and expansion: she must come to appreciate the necessity for concerted social action on earth, beyond the imperatives of her religion for a heavenly salvation. Although in the process Wright intimates that Sue's religion is useless as a cure for earthly social ills, he makes the point that regardless of the extent to which a Southern Negro may uphold his religious belief, he must not confine his fervor to the search for a heavenly reward. Wright does not appear at this point in his life to have been compelled to speak out against the personal value of religious faith. However, religion is not enough, he was saying, if the Negro is to build his paradise on earth—under the auspices of Marx, of course.

Much later, in the 1950s, Wright was armed with Freud, Nietzsche, and the existentialists to engage in battle against formal religions. His long nonfiction in this period repeatedly mirrors Wright's distaste for systematic theology, religious institutions, and prescribed patterns of religious behavior. A whimsical and not-altogether-pleasing product of his late psychological and metaphysical meanderings is a novel, *Savage Holiday*. "A curiously incoherent little potboiler," one critic aptly labeled it, "about which the less said the better."[15] As a work of art, it merits scant attention, for it is faulty in structure and inappropriately melodramatic in plot. Its violence is sensational and seemingly senseless, its serious tone even ludicrous in spots. Because its publication has been limited to cheap paperback editions, *Savage Holiday* may never reach a large segment of the scholarly community—all the better for Wright's artistic reputation.[16] Those few critics who have perused it and then condemned it on aesthetic grounds as a second- or third-rate novel cannot be contradicted. Yet, *Savage Holiday* is an interesting small annex to the larger concerns around which Wright had built so much of his other fiction and nonfiction.

Although occasionally the plot, the reconstructed interior monologues, and the viewpoint of the third-person, omniscient narrator touch the perimeters of broader social ramifications, the novel is basically narrow in scope and theme. It appears to have been inspired by Wright's wish to portray the ill effects of a rigid Protestant background and an unexamined Freudian complex on an unmarried, middle-aged business executive in New York City. Even though Erskine Fowler, the main character, is a white man and no Negroes are represented, the novel cannot be considered a significant example of a shift in Negro writing from racial concerns to wider American and universal themes. *Savage Holiday* is one more item to help complete a psychological and philosophical sketch of an author who already had proven himself capable of creating more profound and more pleasing works of art.

For a better understanding of the Protestant archetypal nature of Erskine Fowler in *Savage Holiday*, excerpts from an essay in Wright's *White Man, Listen!* are useful. The content of that particular section—"Tradition and Industrialization"—is Wright's explanation of the meaning of European traditions and colonialism for African-Asian leaders. Race and racism are the highlighted key issues, but the harmful effects of Christianity are not neglected. After asserting that Calvin and Luther had freed the minds of Western men to develop science and industry and to undertake vast social revolutions, Wright claims that the new Protestant could not fully accept the challenge. Instead, he remained in part the victim of an older sense of guilt and the persistent search for earthly salvation through religious teachings and symbols. However, a "Church world" was slowly transformed into a "worldly world," even though the residue of white racism never disappeared. In spite of his trend toward secularism, the Protestant could never shake off what is best termed the heritage of original sin, and thus could never completely comprehend or adjust to the new freedom offered man.[17] Simplifying his concept of the Protestant, Wright declares:

The Protestant is a queer animal who has never fully understood himself, has never guessed that he is an abortive freeman, an issue of historical birth that never quite came to full life. It has been conveniently forgotten that the Protestant is a product and a result of *oppression*, which might well account for his inability to latch directly onto the Greek heritage. . . . Stripped by the heavy, intolerant conditions of Catholic rule of much of his superfluous emotional baggage, the emerging Protestant rebel, harassed by his enemies and haunted by his own guilt, was doomed to *react* rather than *act*, to *protest* rather than *affirm*. . . . The Protestant is the brave blind man cursed by destiny with a burden which he has not the inner grace to accept wholeheartedly.[18]

Although in *White Man, Listen!* and in *Savage Holiday* Wright chose to confine his remarks to Protestantism, his extended tour of Spain later assured him, as *Pagan Spain* attests, that Catholicism also had fostered a sense of guilt in its own way.

The Protestant theme in *Savage Holiday* may be expanded to include all Christianity—as, in fact, can be done in the passage from *White Man, Listen!* when Nietzsche is recognized as the source for Wright's statements. Nietzsche's *Twilight of the Idols* and especially *The Antichrist* furnish similar explanations for the fallacies and weaknesses of Christianity. To deny Nietzsche a role in the creation of *Savage Holiday* would be to overlook the numerous references to Nietzsche in Wright's nonfiction and the inclusion in *Savage Holiday* of an epigraph from Nietzsche's *Thus Spake Zarathustra*. However, Erskine Fowler is not a version of Nietzsche's "superman." Although at times Fowler does display a certain will to power, he merely "goes under," without ever "getting across." So, the elements of the novel that with some justification may be said to owe their existence to Wright's knowledge of Nietzsche are most workably restricted to the presentation of Christianity as an inhibiting force, detrimental to the ultimate identification of man's free, albeit forlorn, self.

In *Savage Holiday* Wright mixes Nietzsche with Freud—a not-implausible blend. He first suggests the connection in an epigraph to Part I from Freud's *Totem and Taboo*: "in the very nature of a holiday there is excess; the holiday mood is brought about by the release of what is forbidden."[19] During the sixty-or-so hours spanned by the narrative, Erskine Fowler's actions are plainly attributed to a Freudian complex; and his inability to admit to, and also adjust to, the nature of his complex is associated with the constraining qualities inherent in his Protestant personality. Rather than to examine the dark and dreadful contents of his nightmarish subconscious mind, Fowler has been encouraged by his religion to look to the cross and to the Bible for guidance in overcoming both the horrible desires often surging outward from his inner world and the temptations toward sins of the flesh occasionally intruding from the external world. When near the novel's conclusion, in a rare fit of willfullness, Fowler strips naked the enticing, symbolic mother figure, Mabel Blake, he at last permits his Freudian neurosis to burst the bounds of his Protestant restraint. He then assumes a one-sided role of Nietzsche's superman—the best known and, when treated alone, the most erroneously interpreted side—that of the man of will who follows his instincts. However, when he brutally slays Mabel, Fowler is no longer cast in the superman mold, for he has abandoned that artful control over will and instinct so critical to the proper composure of Nietzsche's superman. Instead, Fowler has been victimized by his Protestant training. He has been taught to suppress his ugly love-hate mother complex and to rely on a combination of hard, honest, secular labor and pious Christian belief to soothe guilt feelings that arise from his sensing the distance between the inner man of evil desires and the outer man of good Christian works. At the end of the novel, Wright intends Fowler's crime to be a tragic testimony to Christianity's failure to develop stable personalities from man's chaotic internal life, further disturbed by the inculcation of Christian guilt, itself a by-product of the concept of original sin.

Savage Holiday, then, combines strands from Freud and Nietzsche, but only after it has made a faulty start in the direction of a larger social commentary. Nearly a half of Part I of the three-part novel is devoted to a detailed rendering of the circumstances that have set Fowler free to shape a new life, within the bounds of his Christian beliefs, of course. Although much is revealed in this section about Fowler's personality and physical appearance, the events and their settings of a Saturday-night scene inexcusably mislead the reader to expect an entirely different narrative, one filled with Fowler's plottings and revenge against the Longevity Life Insurance Company. At age forty-three, thirty of those years having been spent climbing the company ladder, Fowler discovers that he has been pressured into retirement to make room for the president's son, who will be the Manhattan district manager. These facts are not disclosed until Wright has painstakingly de-

scribed a banquet in honor of Fowler. We also learn that
Fowler is a Mason, a Rotarian, a Sunday school superin-
tendent, a man of hard-earned means—in short, all that
adds up to a small-town Babbitt rather than a New York
City executive. Physically he is tall, muscular, hulking, with
deep-set brown eyes, jet-black bushy hair, and a jut-
ting lower jaw—imposing but almost grotesque (Wright
departs from the stereotype of the fair, blue-eyed Anglo-
Saxon Protestant). Deliberating over the series of em-
barrassing and frustrating events that have forced him to
leave the company with a lifetime pension for his quiet cooperation, Fowler departs the banquet hall and plunges
into the gay Saturday-night city crowds, vowing future
revenge against Longevity Life, its president, the president's
son, and a nasty vice-president.

At this point in Part I, Wright abrogates his apparent
promise for a socially oriented naturalistic novel. The expected examination of the ethics of a large white-collar
organization is superceded. In its place he substitutes a
psychologically oriented detective story. The banquet scene
and Fowler's mental flashbacks are not, however, wholly
useless for the remainder of the novel; for Wright uses them
to intimate that Fowler, when under emotional stress, un-
dergoes a subconscious contact with a disconcerting frag-
ment from his past. By touching the ends of four automatic
colored pencils inside his coat pocket, he placates a haunting image:

Whenever he was distraught or filled with anxiety, he
invariably made this very same compulsive gesture which he
had developed in some obscure and forgotten crisis . . . ; his
touching those pencils always somehow reassured him, for
they seemed to symbolize an inexplicable need to keep
contact with some emotional resolution whose meaning
and content he did not know.[20]

Not until the end of *Savage Holiday*, after Mabel Blake has been murdered by Fowler and he has turned himself over to the police, does he recognize the inner horror that he has been shielding from his consciousness. Meanwhile, during his abbreviated company-imposed holiday, he is drawn closer to a self-recognition about his hidden internal life. That his reactions end in uncontrollable violence underscores how one irrational force, Christianity, has not prepared Fowler to cope with another irrational force, the components of his psyche.

Fowler's path to both revelation and tragedy is not a long one, for the whole plot is decided in a mere two-and-a-half days. The drama is overly intense in this respect. Following an established trait of his fiction, Wright rapidly focuses on Fowler's consciousness, leaving to the edges of the novel the shallow and undeveloped characters of the few other figures. After the banquet, Fowler goes to his tenth-floor apartment. He thinks about five-year-old Tony Blake, the only son of Fowler's widowed neighbor, Mabel, whose husband had been killed near the end of World War II. The constant ringing of Mabel's phone reminds Fowler that she is rarely at home because she works at night. He reflects, however, that she does find time to see many male suitors, all to the neglect of the unhappy Tony. Early the next morning Fowler's uneasy sleep is interrupted by Tony's drum-beating in the hall, which abruptly terminates a dream in which a falling tree in a forest is about to crash down upon Fowler's head. The dream itself is filled with all sorts of contrived Freudian symbols.

The succeeding events in the story are swift and, when viewed from a distance, farcical, although they are replete with physical and psychological tragedy. Fowler thinks about his past—about the death of his father when Fowler was only three and then the shame of being baited by other children for having a mother who was a prostitute, who, in fact, later spent two years in prison and died soon thereafter. One Freudian dimension is added to another when Fowler realizes that Mabel Blake, "alone, sensual, impulsive," is so much like the retained image of his own mother.[21] Quickly abandoning such an idea because of its obvious implications, he steps into the hall to fetch his Sunday paper. Unfortunately, the door slams shut and locks behind him, and, worse yet, Fowler is nude. A frenzied attempt either to return to his apartment or to hide from other occupants of the building ensues. As a result of his straight-laced Protestant background, he is unable to face the possible embarrassment of exposing himself to anyone who might help him. He travels up and down in elevators and frantically through hallways, hoping that some miracle will occur. At last he bursts out into an open balcony where Tony Blake is playing on an electric hobbyhorse. Fowler's momentum carries him toward Tony who, frightened by the nude man, falls backward toward the railing, failing to reach for assistance. Instead, Tony plunges ten floors to his death. From this accidental and dramatic incident begins Fowler's involvement with Mabel.

Fowler manages to enter his room unnoticed, but now must carry the burden of responsibility for Tony's death. Not revealing to anyone his part in the accident, he goes off to the Mt. Ararat Church to teach Sunday school, for which he is late for the first time in ten years. Later, in the repose of Central Park, he reviews the succession of events and concludes not that he has committed a crime but that Mabel has been guilty of neglecting her son and of putting fear into him by allowing him to watch her periodic "fights" —her sexual encounters with men. Obviously, then, Mabel has received a punishment through the will of God, and God has used Fowler as one of his instruments. Nevertheless, Fowler cannot dispel a nagging sense of guilt. He soon comes to believe that "he must somehow redeem what had happened to Tony," for by "redeeming Tony, he'd be redeeming himself."[22] The form of redemption is to be hardly a traditionally Christian one, because it clashes head on with Fowler's Freudian mother complex.

By Monday morning Fowler has struck up a condescending relationship with the twenty-nine-year-old Mabel. Assuming a role of friend and protector, he decides to help with the funeral arrangements for Tony. In Mabel's apartment he is attracted to her voluptuous manner, and he senses the beginnings of a strong emotion toward her. Suddenly, like a bolt from the beyond, complicated pieces begin to fit together for him:

One act on his part could tie into a knot of meaning all of the contradictory impulses evoked in him by this dramatically sensual woman; *one* decision . . . could allay his foolish guilt about Tony's strange death; *one* gesture . . . could quell the riot of those returning memories from the dark bog of his childhood past; . . . *one* vow could enable him to answer God's call, save this woman, and serve Him as he should—*He'd ask her to marry him!*[23]

As for the rest of *Savage Holiday*, it is an account of Fowler's attempts to win over not only the love but also the whole being of Mabel, so that his guilt feelings would disappear. There are touching moments in taxicabs and New York restaurants, but by the end of the evening—much is compacted into a short time—Fowler has become jealous of Mabel's male friends, who happen to appear in restaurants or to telephone Mabel's apartment while Fowler is there. At one point he calls her a whore; at another he contritely reveals to her his part in Tony's death. As for Mabel, she will not be overwhelmed by Fowler's sudden and unexpected assault upon the sexual freedom she has apparently enjoyed. Furthermore, she assists Wright in tying together a Freudian thread when she informs Fowler,

"You need a mother."[24] Late in the evening, a verbal battle ensues, and Fowler is shocked to learn that Mabel has never really loved Tony. Deep from Fowler's subconscious emerges a picture of his mother, whom he suspects never cared for him. When, finally, Mabel agrees to marry Fowler, but then insists that her sexual affairs be her own business and threatens to walk out on him, his subconscious hatred for his own prostitute mother, who had neglected her son's needs while engaging in her trade, is transformed into a hatred for Mabel, the mother figure. Thus ensues a brutal butcher-knife slaughter of Mabel at the hands of Fowler.

Although by now Wright seems to have more than made his point about the good Christian who suddenly goes beserk, he must heavy-handedly complete the design suggested by the Freudian materials introduced in the opening banquet scene. So it is that when Fowler calmly looks into his bathroom mirror after his beastly deed, he recalls a scene from his childhood in which he had beaten and crushed a girl companion's doll, for "the doll was his mother and he had 'killed' her because all the boys had said that his mother was bad."[25] The Freudian-explained movement of the novel, then, has been from mother to doll to Mabel, and the childhood symbolic act has finally been completed in an adult symbolic act. However, Wright adds a final irony: after Fowler has turned himself over to the police and while he is undergoing interrogation, he is stunned by a new revelation—he actually had never "killed" the doll; he had merely drawn on paper with colored pencils the figure of a shattered mother-figure doll! And for this reason his automatic pencils offer him security in times of emotional stress, for they have been the subconscious reminders of a foul deed never committed.

For the sake of Wright's literary reputation, *Savage Holiday* would best be left untouched between its sensational paperback covers. However, for a fuller picture of the influences on Wright's thinking, especially during his residence in France, the novel is valuable, even if painfully so. Although it focuses on the irrational aspects of man's mind and the irrational mode of his behavior, it also suggests that the irrational has a rational explanation. Possibly too, in the case of Fowler, his violent and destructive actions would never have occurred had his mother given him the love he craved and needed and, correlatively, had she not tramped off with many men in her sexual abandonment. There is a temptation, of course, to extrapolate further and to call Wright a moral Puritan; however, the bulk of his writings would not substantiate such a theory.[26] *Savage Holiday* is, then, a poorly constructed, too-seriously articulated, overstated work, purposely employing Freudian devices and a few ideas from Nietzsche. It neatly fits the pattern of Wright's attitudes toward Christianity, and it may be linked to the rationalist impulses behind the type of humanism he seems to have been formulating sometime after he had left the United States.

In France, Wright circulated among the existentialists. Whether his involvement with them should be equated with a belief in the complex tenets of existentialism is another matter (Webb's biography of Wright is not useful in this respect). *The Outsider* does reflect Wright's conscious use of existential thought. Within a framework of existential ideas, that novel seems to have evolved from two earlier works, *Native Son* and "The Man Who Lived Underground." All three center upon a single figure who operates within existential concepts. In *Native Son*, Bigger Thomas is a prototype for an existential hero, imagined by Wright when he had not yet been consciously motivated by existential philosophical presuppositions. The anonymous main character in "The Man Who Lived Underground," created by Wright before his associations with the French existentialists, is almost a purely existential hero. Cross Damon in *The Outsider* is an existentialist who is propelled to an ugly extreme by Wright in order to uncover existentialism's logical but socially disastrous outcome.

Native Son is most clearly read and understood as a wrathful commentary on American Negro-white relations. It has often fascinated critics in its possibilities for being less specific and more universal than it seems.[27] Certain recurring words in the novel can be related to the ideas and the terminology in much existential writing; for instance, "alienation," "despair," and "freedom" abound. Even the titles of the novel's three sections—"Fear," "Flight," and "Fate"—resemble common existential language. However, the question must be asked whether the language, when it is stripped from the narrative concerns of race relations and Marxism, can in itself sustain an existential metaphysical design.

In an explanatory essay that followed the publication of *Native Son*, Wright states that Bigger "through some quirk of circumstance . . . had become estranged from the religion and folk culture of his race."[28] The "quirk of circumstance," however, is plainly illustrated within the novel. Early scenes portray the crowded conditions in which the Thomas family must try to survive in their apartment in Chicago's Black Belt. The tensions that have been generated within their one room partially stem from the condition itself. In addition there is a taut personal gap between Bigger and his family. He resents the fact that they have quietly accepted their misery and exclusion from the wider society. He displays toward them "an attitude of iron reserve" and communicates with them from "behind a wall, a curtain."[29] After Mary Dalton's death and Bigger's return home, he mentally reviews at the breakfast table what his mother, sister, and brother individually represent in terms

of their resignation to being assigned to the black subculture
of America. He feels that their path cannot be his; he senses
that his personality would be doomed.[30] Later, after he has
been trapped and jailed, he reacts in much the same way
to his family and to his companions during their visits with
him. Their sense of shame repulses him. He cannot understand why they do not comprehend that his bloody rebellion has symbolized what every black man wants desperately to perform against the white world. *"They ought to be
glad!"* he thinks: "Had he not taken fully upon himself the
crime of being black? Had he not done the thing which they
dreaded above all others?"[31]

Despite the fact that Bigger often seems ready to extend
his thoughts upward to a metaphysical level, he usually returns to the realities of the bleak existence that the whites
are forcing upon him in his particular social environment.
His alienation from his family and his friends is the result
not of a higher and more tragic truth but, rather, of the
socially unfavorable traits of his personality that have developed out of the inner frustrations and rages caused by
his sensitivity to his exclusion from the larger society
around him. When he first journeys to the Dalton house,
he must carry a knife and a gun, so that he can somehow
feel an equality with white power, and thus be endowed
with "a sense of completeness."[32] Only after his accidental
killing of Mary Dalton do his weapons become unimportant. His act has raised him into the white world. Here
he receives attention, albeit in the form of a reinforced
white hate and fear. It is not a state of existential alienation
that Bigger is trying to attain. He wants, instead, to establish a human link—one man to another—that he thinks
should rationally exist exclusive of the artificial barrier of
skin color.

Wright's indelicate insertion of Marxist propaganda in
the last section of the novel is not altogether unfitting.

Marxism, in the abstract, assumes that meaningful bonds among men are possible. The goals of Marxism are seemingly consistent with the nature of Bigger's search—"to merge himself with others and be a part of this world."[33] However, because Bigger's role in the novel is symbolically greater than that of a mere economic pawn in a capitalistic system, Marxism becomes too narrow, too simple, for an appropriate conclusion to his journey. And because Bigger's strivings are clearly within the realm of social goals, in fact within a framework of belief that relatedness is possible among men, existentialism as a philosophical explanation for his desires and actions is overly broad. Yet, remove Wright's attitude that after Marxism there is nothing to resolve Bigger's problems, and what remains is an existential void reflected in the final pages of the novel. There Bigger faces his death having discovered no new truth in Marxism or no abiding conviction that the two murders he has been involved in are either socially wrong or philosophically immoral. On the one hand, Wright has built his novel within the area of purely social concerns; on the other, he has suspended it on a note of ambiguity, which, if combined with the language of despair in the novel, is logically extensible into the existential darkness.

Wright's treatment of religion, as mirrored in Bigger's beliefs, is another facet of *Native Son* that easily lends itself to existential propositions. Although Bigger is placed outside the folk religion of his people, Wright intends ostensibly to show how Christianity is an ally to a larger exploitative plot against the Negro. In this respect, especially striking is a grotesque scene in which a captive Bigger is confronted by a Ku Klux Klan cross, flaming atop a building behind an enraged and hostile white mob. Naturally, the paradox between the symbolic offering of salvation for all men and the hateful motivation behind the burning of the cross is quickly grasped by Bigger, and he flings to the ground a cross given to him earlier by a priest. It is not religion but the hypocrisy accompanying Christianity that he is disavowing.

The particular rather than the general nature of this act is reinforced later in the jail during an interview between Bigger and his Marxist lawyer, Max. Bigger says that he no longer could attend church services after he had realized that the singing, shouting, and praying of his black kin "didn't get 'em nothing," because, apparently, "the white folks got everything." Furthermore, the idea of Christianity as part of the white scheme for controlling Negro behavior is strengthened when Bigger claims that "the white folks like for us to be religious, then they can do what they want with us." Bigger thus is not in rebellion against the concept of the existence of a God. His alienation from formal religion is inspired by social, not metaphysical, awareness. Even here an ambiguity arises. Pressed by the questioning Max, Bigger reveals that he is not sure that a God exists, and that after he is strapped into the electric chair and the current is turned on, he will perish "for always."[34] Again, Wright has forced the novel beyond the limits of social protest into the area of metaphysical implications.

In many ways, then, *Native Son* is a perplexing novel. Because of Wright's obtrusive pro-Marxism and because of the predominant theme of protest against a particular social injustice, it defies an easy categorization into purely existential literature. The protest in *Native Son* asks that social changes occur. It also implies that man can bring them about. To the degree that existentialism views man as set free from the claims of a God, Wright also perceives man's position as such. When Bigger meets his death not in despair but with a belief that he has at last been able to acquire a new freedom by shaping his own destiny— though through violence and killing—he symbolizes an authorial tenet that man's freedom is within his grasp, here on earth, if he is willing to accept the responsibility and consequences for it. The message is an existential one; but it does mirror the same social, not metaphysical, concerns and protests that powerfully emerge from *Black Boy*. Wright seems to have reverted to attitudes of his boyhood and adolescence—rationalism and agnostic humanism—the latent concepts underlying the final words in *Black Boy*:

I headed North, full of a hazy notion that life could be lived with dignity, that the personalities of others should not be violated, that men should be able to confront other men without fear or shame, and that if men were lucky in their living on earth they might win some redeeming meaning for their having struggled and suffered here beneath the stars.[35]

In *Native Son*, Marxism offers the pseudo-scientific, rational plan for achieving that meaning; and Bigger Thomas must remain only an ambiguous and shadowy prefigurement of the pronouncedly existential, anonymous antihero in "The Man Who Lived Underground."

Perhaps Wright's disillusionment with the Communist Party in the early 1940s and his resultant depressed state of mind caused him to write "The Man Who Lived Underground."[36] Or perhaps he was beginning to mold a new and cynical personal philosophy conceived from his interpretations of works by such men as Dostoyevsky and Nietzsche. More feasibly though, for the first time in print, Wright was allowing those usually transitory pessimistic moments in his public thinking—caused primarily by his observations of what he considered the profoundly irrational behavior of the white world toward Negroes—to enter a story and then to be carried to a conclusion consistent with the prevailing attitude in the work. Regardless, the existential materials buried in *Native Son* for the imagination to discover and expand are plainly evident in "The Man Who Lived Underground."

Critical comments about this lengthy short story have varied. Different interpreters have chosen different aspects to praise or deprecate. Irving Howe, for example, talks about style and commends Wright for combining a naturalistic style with a radical projective image—a Negro trapped in a sewer.[37] The direction of his remarks is toward the racial problem. Saunders Redding calls the story "an impressive failure," in which "no passion has meaning, no insight is revealed, no idea truly conveyed, no theme made unmistakably plain."[38] In a comparison of the story and Ralph Ellison's *Invisible Man* to works by Dostoyevsky, Herbert Hill suggests that Wright's work is a much greater accomplishment than Redding is willing to acknowledge. He feels that the tale exemplifies Wright's "great concern with meaning, with identity, and with the necessity to remain sane in a society where the individual personality is denied and the world appears devoid of meaning."[39] In this statement Hill accentuates the existential qualities of "The Man Who Lived Underground," but he underrates the pessimistic tone of the story. He has, however, probed deeply, finding some meaning in the very presence of meaninglessness. The fact that the story's main character articulates no meaning from what he has lived through is not an indication that the tale has conveyed nothing. In its nothingness rests its existential content, although Hill has not named it as such and naturally has not branded the existentialism of a particular sort.

The racial aspects of "The Man Who Lived Underground" may be dismissed (as they often are in interpretations of *The Outsider*), but not without an argument. No doubt race helps to move the plot. The anonymous central figure of the story—hereafter referred to as "Man"—is a hostage of underground passages and sewers because he has had to elude the police from whom he has escaped, after being wrongly accused of killing a white woman. That the police had arraigned him in the first place is a result of their frenzied predilection for apprehending the most likely suspects, that is, Negroes. However, once Wright has located his black man in the underground, specific references to, and actions around, racial topics cease. Even when Man peeps into a basement Negro church where services are being conducted, his mind moves from a consideration of the worshiping and singing Negroes to a contemplation of an almost innate sense of guilt that he has identified in most men. A situation that suggests meaning in a particular social realm is thus quickly projected into a wider metaphysical range, and the racial theme is replaced with overtones that are universally applicable.

The problems of self-identity and the search for meaning in the world are, as Hill has noted, thematic focal points in the story. Associated with them, and woven into the composition of the narrative, are the relationships between cause and effect and between appearance and reality. Posed also is the question of whether man can achieve real communication with others. Like Ellison's *Invisible Man*, "The Man Who Lived Underground" soars in its subject matter far above a specific social condition. In both pieces the presence of an unnamed Negro central character immediately endows the works with one level of meaning, while the generalized themes surge outward. From Wright, at least, the implications are not optimistic ones, either for Man or for mankind.

Man has escaped into the underground of the world, symbolically the underground of the mind. There he builds a cave-home, which he periodically leaves in order to view the outside world of people who seemingly are socially interrelating with one another. Having been senselessly tortured and beaten by the police, he strives to discover whether what he sees from his peepholes and his disguised forays will fit a consistent, rational pattern—whether what has happened to him in the world is part of a larger truth or merely an unpleasant exception. However, a truth or a pattern is never found—here again is an exposition of the existential paradox that meaninglessness is its own meaning. Moreover, Man causes effects in the world above him, the sources for which are unseen and unknown by the people there. He himself becomes a contributor to the undesign of mankind, adding chaos to chaos. At one point, after stealing money, jewels, appliances, tools, even electric power from the outside world, thus mimicking the deeds performed by those he has clandestinely spied upon, Man questions the objective validity of moral schemes: "Maybe *any*thing's right. . . . Yes, if the world as men had made it was right, then anything else was right, any act a man took to satisfy himself, murder, theft, torture."[40] This view possibly is a conscious extension of the Nietzschean idea that moral schemes should be individual, not collective. Man does eventually subscribe to it. As he silently watches other people receiving punishments for deeds he himself has performed—a sadistic reversal of the circumstances that had forced him to flee to the underground—he transforms into a universal quality pertinent even to himself the sense of guilt he earlier had assigned to other people and not necessarily to himself. He has observed and sensed his own participation in the injustices of the world. He has been the agent for an irrational chain of events leading not only to suffering but also to a suicide. Man has helped to lead the world deeper into the darkness of an existential universe protracted to its ambiguous logical-illogical, rational-irrational limit, that is, Man has heaped destruction upon destruction, chaos upon chaos.

Under the burden of his own guilt and a renewed feeling

of responsibility to the world, Man becomes anxious to leave his hole "to go somewhere and say something to somebody."[41] He wants to explain his experience to the outside world. It is important for everyone, he thinks. The earlier sights of guilty people in the church, of movie patrons unwittingly laughing at their doubles on the screen, of an abandoned and dead baby pushed along amid sewage—all had "some dim meaning" linking them together, "some magical relationship" making them kin; all were convincing him that, "with their tongueless reality," they were "striving to tell him something."[42] The message is not clear, but he is instilled with a boisterous gaiety. Here Wright seems on the verge of pointing to the existential position that comprehends man free from meaning because there is no meaning, man free to shape his world because the fetters of past fictitious meanings based on meaninglessness are understood for what they are. On this premise, though for him an unconscious one, Man plunges happily into the open air, intent on communicating his story and urgently hoping that other men will detect the essence of his underground experience.

Man fatally discovers that communication is impossible. Herein is the overriding pessimistic outlook in "The Man Who Lived Underground." Man ecstatically seeks out the policemen who had earlier tortured him. When he finds them, he wants to embrace them in a display of friendship and brotherhood, but he is rebuked. Furthermore, while he leads them to the scenes of his experiences and recounts for them the steps in his vision, he learns in the cruelest manner—through death—that they will not and cannot understand him. A manhole cover closes over him and he flows with the filth of the sewer, a lethal bullet lodged in his dimming memory. An optimistic existential freedom never penetrates the dark possibility in the existential view, and Man is rushed along in the wake of the story's hopelessness, "a whirling object . . . alone in the darkness, veering, tossing, lost in the heart of the earth."[43] He perishes for no rational reason, just as, Wright implies, the larger Man lives and dies for no purpose in a world without purposes. Herein lies a fate far unlike that of Sue who, at the end of "Bright and Morning Star," has offered her life for *the* cause, Marxism, in the trust and hope of a new and dignified freedom under the aegis of a political star.

"The Man Who Lived Underground" marks a low and pessimistic point in the philosophical props beneath Wright's publications. The unconsciously existential materials are transported to the brink of an ebullient and optimistic vision of man's future and then are collapsed with a blast of despair. Somewhere between the years of *Native Son* and *The Outsider*—roughly between 1940 and 1953 —Wright's vision of life was undergoing changes. His decision to live in France is a manifest outcome of this process. The publication date of *Black Boy* falls, however, within that period. Because Wright's optimistic flight to the American North concludes the autobiography, and because *Black Boy* combines both protest and a belief that rational minds in the white and black worlds could conceivably live together in relative harmony with personal dignity, a contradiction may have been developing in Wright's thinking. We must remember, though, that the autobiography is a retelling of past events and reactions and covers Wright's life only up to 1927. Furthermore, *Black Boy* is composed of many sections written and published much earlier than 1945.

In only one brief spot does the autobiography cast doubt upon man's ability to mold a rational world. Significantly, these remarks are injected parenthetically, as though they were entered as afterthoughts applicable to Wright's current beliefs during the mid-1940s and certainly not to his attitudes during his adolescence. Complaining that Negroes have never been allowed "to catch the full spirit of Western civilization," Wright parenthetically examines what he thinks is a lack of kindness, tenderness, and passion in American Negro culture. Then he advances beyond the social perimeter of his prior concerns:

(When I brooded upon the cultural barrenness of black life, I wondered if clean, positive tenderness, love, honor, loyalty, and the capacity to remember were native with man. I asked myself if these human qualities were not fostered, won, struggled and suffered for, preserved in ritual from one generation to another.) [44]

The implicit doubts of the final statement are closer to the controlling philosophy worked out within "The Man Who Lived Underground" than that in *Native Son* or other of Wright's publications during his affiliation with the Communist Party. Although a vein of protest pervaded his short stories and novels of that time, it was a protest that pleaded with white America to change its ways and its society. The keystone of Wright's beliefs then was a faith in man's rational powers. Later, in the mid- and late-1950s, his nonfiction affirmed a similar foundation of thought, tempered somewhat by misgivings about the tremendous inroads already made by irrational forces in the world. Somewhere between the period of his Party activities and of his late nonfiction, Wright either was so moved toward temporarily accepting a wholly pessimistic viewpoint or had become so depressed, perhaps by the continuing discouraging history of American Negro-white relations, that he found it impossible to resolve optimistically "The Man Who Lived Underground." He did return in subsequent publications to his former optimistic, humanistic view, even in works written from his self-exile in France, where, as one of his friends has suggested, a new sense of freedom and a favorable literary reception "in some ways fulfilled him as a social being."[45] And despite the apparent despair and hopelessness of *The Outsider*—written so near in time to his late nonfiction—that novel ends on a paradoxical note that reestablished the hopeful and humanistic basis of Wright's thinking.

In recent years *The Outsider* has received as much scholarly attention as any of Wright's books. Because existentialism has become a modern substitute for older theological systems and has been the guiding philosophy behind much post-World War II Western fiction, literary criticism naturally has had increasingly to interpret existential writing. *The Outsider* has gained attention more because of the category it falls into than because of any aesthetic merits. The artistic qualities of the novel have been attacked often enough, the main objections being that the themes are painfully reiterated and that the long sections of philosophical dialogue are both tedious and unnecessary.[46] However, perceptive analyses have been fashioned in terms of the existentialism in the novel.[47] Two viewpoints have developed: one treats the whole of *The Outsider* as a consistent working out of existential tenets; the other, more plausible viewpoint attempts to show how the novel ironically rejects the nihilistic-existential premises of the hero, Cross Damon. Although the French existentialism that influenced Wright by way of Sartre and Camus is perplexingly ambiguous in its own right, the novel adds a few more complications. Such matters in the novel as the role of race, the purpose of apparently gratuitous violence, and the use of contrived coincidence in plot are difficult to resolve. Unfortunately, the line between aesthetic and philosophic judgments is easily blurred. Furthermore, Cross Damon may be interpreted through both Nietzscheism and French existentialism, thus expanding the problems on the philosophical level alone. Another complicating factor is the question whether Wright himself fully understood the philosophical materials he was employing.

The least controversial interpretation of *The Outsider* is that it represents Cross Damon's search for meaning and for values in a world where he assumes there is no God and where "man is nothing in particular."[48] Cross eventually dies, having found neither meaning nor values—or so it would appear. His seeming predicament is compounded when, after he has committed four murders and has been directly responsible for two other deaths, he whispers in his dying moment, "In my heart . . . I'm innocent."[49] He has found no ultimate standard by which his actions may be judged. Though Cross enters the novel with a belief that life is meaningless, he does embark on a journey for self-identity, supposedly in respect to a more positive philosophy than his nihilistic existentialism. Meaninglessness apparently is not enough; it is too negative to fulfill the identity he craves. Wright stresses the theme of identity by placing Cross in situations where it is imperative that he assume aliases. At one time or another Cross is Brown, Charles Webb, Addison Jordan, John Clark, or Lionel Lane. His own name is related also to the themes; for "Cross" suggests, as one critic has stated, "the hero's god-like desire to be the autonomous and self-enclosed martyr," whereas "Damon" symbolizes his demoniacal qualities.[50]

The major themes in *The Outsider* are clear: the quests for meaning, values, and identity in a world lacking a God and apparent meaning. With the exception of the interpretation prompted by Cross's constant name-changing, all the themes are outlined specifically in various dialogues or through Wright's third-person, omniscient narration of the monologues carried on in Cross's mind. The heavy-handed reiteration of these themes contributes to the unfavorable critical judgments rendered by reviewers and scholars. It does, however, provide some certainty amid the ambiguities and paradoxes inherent within the novel's existential frame of reference.

The Outsider is about a Negro who is meant to be more than a Negro. Some critics feel, as Morris Beja does, that "the overwhelming cause" for Cross's alienation "is, as a matter of fact, his color."[51] At the literal level, as another critic suggests, Cross's physical blackness and the resentful self-hatred that may have resulted in part from being a Negro provide a practical image to embody the darkness of existential dread.[52] Certainly, Cross's race does advance the plot at many points. Cross himself takes advantage of the whites' stereotyped image of the stupid and grinning Negro in order to obtain a duplicate of a dead man's birth certificate from the white public officials in the Newark, New Jersey, City Hall. He is then able to offer paper proof that he is a Lionel Lane. The Communist Party employs him in New York to draw public attention to the larger social and economic issues behind the problems and conflicts in Negro-white relations. Even Ely Houston, the New York district attorney who is an outsider of sorts because he is hunchbacked, is fascinated by Cross. He sympathizes with the position of an outsider that Cross has been forced into because of his race. Only later, near the end of the novel, does Houston perceive a deeper kinship with Cross for philosophical reasons not dependent upon race. The Communist Party, too, does not comprehend Cross for what he is until Party leaders have abandoned their tendency to catalogue him as a Negro. So, ironically, the novel is extended because of Cross's blackness, as he consciously exploits stereotyped racial attitudes in order to survive.

Cross himself feels detached from and suspended above race. He thinks, for instance, that his Negro acquaintances in the Chicago post office are "outside of his life . . . and that his problem was one of the relationship of himself to himself."[53] He wants to communicate with other "rebels" —people who are "outsiders not because they had been born black and poor, but because they had thought their way through the many veils of illusion" in the world.[54] Cross, then, is proposed by Wright to be a man having "no myths, no tradition, no race."[55] Race is not intended to be the center for thematic materials. Though his readers might be predisposed to associate existentialism with the life experiences of many American Negroes, Wright apparently is not.

As in *Native Son*, the plot and setting in *The Outsider* begin on a wintry day in Chicago, though the black-on-white motif is not maintained throughout the latter. Cross Damon's occupation as a post-office clerk reflects that of Jake Jackson in *Lawd Today*. Like Jake, too, Cross has marital problems, which are complicated by Cross's affair with a fifteen-year-old girl who is now apparently pregnant. In addition, Cross and his wife, Gladys, have three boys of their own. His marital problems are exposed early in the novel, through mental flashbacks. Also established quickly are the philosophical and psychological turmoils constantly taking place within Cross. From his mother's strict Protestant religion he has acquired, without a corresponding belief in a God-savior, a sense of dread that accompanies the presence of a Protestant God, whose "awful face" is shaped "in the form of a huge and crushing NO." Although Cross's rebellion against this God has been philosophical, it has also been influenced by his "unbridled hunger for the sensual."[56] He has not been able to destroy the guilt feeling apparently prevalent in the Western world and identified by Nietzsche, for instance, but he has retained certain traits of Nietzsche's man of instinct. A partially educated intellectual, Cross is familiar with the literature of the irrational—Heidegger, Dostoyevsky, Nietzsche, etc.—and subscribes to, as "the fondest and deepest conviction of his life," a concept that all men are free to construct their own futures.[57] He is, then, his own God. He theoretically can do what he wants and can pass private judgment on his actions; but before he can use his "lonely will" to map out his life, he must find the answer to an "awful question"— "What's a man?"[58]

A subway accident helps to untangle Cross from the maze of the domestic problems and tensions he daily must face. He escapes the accident unharmed, the dead body of a less fortunate passenger later being mistakenly identified as Cross. Sustained by an eight-hundred-dollar loan that he should have given to his wife, Cross is free to leave Chicago, but not before witnessing his own funeral. Soon he finds it necessary to kill one of his friends who has recognized him in a cheap Chicago hotel. To preserve his freedom from the grips of social obligations, he has had to destroy a life. He then boards a train for New York, very much "afraid of himself," realizing "that to see was not to control, that self-understanding was far short of self-mastery."[59] The echoes from Nietzsche are obvious. A would-be Nietzschean man of will and instinct, Cross knows he is unfulfilled. He also dreads that he must be responsible for himself and his actions in an existential world in which man is "nothing in particular" and has been freed from the past and from the mystical beliefs and values of his culture.

On the train to New York, sheer circumstance again proves significant for Cross. He meets Father Seldon, a Catholic priest who is secure within a preordained system of good and evil. Father Seldon is contrasted with Cross, who must discover "what was good or evil through his own actions" and who believes that "this life . . . was all he had and would ever have."[60] Cross's later chance meeting with Ely Houston, the New York district attorney, leads to lengthy discussions in which they analyze the false props set under societies to prevent their transformations into lawless and disorderly jungles. Houston serves to validate the universal nature of those drives and instincts which Cross senses within himself. Through Houston and Father Seldon, Wright reinforces and clarifies the concepts that Cross believes in. Then Wright adds Bob Hunter, a Negro Pullman-car waiter and a Communist Party member who has entered the country illegally from Trinidad. Through Hunter, Cross makes his way into the Party. Thus, the plot begins to become a mixture of specific political motifs and universal themes.

The passage on which the meaning of *The Outsider* turns is inserted at the point when Cross's beliefs and the nature of his search have been solidly established. Where his beliefs and search might lead has already been illustrated through his murder of his friend and his flight from responsibilities to others in Chicago. Now in New York, apparently a free man with money enough to keep himself for a while, Cross perceptively surveys his predicament, as reported by the narrative voice:

He was without a name, a past, or future; no promises or pledges bound him to those about him. He had to become human before he could mingle again with people. Yet he needed those people and could become human only with them. Dimly he realized that his dilemma, though personal, bore the mark of the general. The lives of children, too, could become human only by growing up with human beings.[61]

From this point to the end of the novel, Wright depicts not how it is impossible for a man to become human, but rather, how it is impossible for Cross to humanize himself through self-control and self-mastery. A connection is plausible between this quoted passage and the epigraph to the final chapter of *The Outsider*, quoted from Nietzsche: "Man is the only being who makes promises." When the dying Cross says to Houston near the end of the novel that "man is a promise that he must never break," Wright himself has passed judgment upon Cross and upon the nihilistic-existential philosophy that has so handily been projected by Cross to chaos and destruction.[62] The diabolical role of the Nietzschean man has been played out by Cross to its logical conclusion, with no regard to that side of Nietzsche's philosophy which reflects a pervasive sentimentality and a need-wish for a community of men. Cross's tragedy is not that he is innocent but that he has been prompted by his unbridled passions to shape a world only for himself.

On his deathbed Cross prefaces his remarks to Houston about man's being a promise to himself with a revelation that undermines the nihilistic-existential precepts he has used to rationalize his actions: "The search can't be done alone. . . . Never alone. . . . Alone man is nothing."[63] Wright seems to be intimating that the individual cannot be the sole source of his own values, if he and society should expect to discover or to create an order in or for the universe. A community of men with a community of interests must be the starting point. To begin with only the individual in mind is to end in violation of a larger humanity—as Cross comes to realize after acknowledging the bloody trail he has left behind him: "He knew that he had cynically scorned, wantonly violated every commitment that civilized men owe, in terms of common honesty and sacred honor, to those with whom they live. That, in essence was his crime."[64] In effect, Wright is exposing a personal belief that sets him apart from much of the nihilistic-existential material that informs the novel.

Before his death Cross's experiences in New York consist of one violent act after another. He joins the Communist Party not out of belief but from a need to hide his past through a new social connection. However, he learns that he must contend with power-seeking men and groups who would control his destiny. His brutal double slaying of the Communist Gil Blount and the neo-fascist Langley Herndon is a reaction to organized attempts at interference with his freedom. When Cross murders Jack Hilton, head of the New York Party, he destroys not only the man who threatens to use against him evidence of the previous murders, but also a symbol of organized intrusions from the outside world. Later, in a lengthy dialogue with the Party theoretician Blimin (discussed in part at the end of Chapter 2 in this study), Cross unmasks the Party for what he feels it is: an exploiter of the people of the twentieth century, who are being cut away by science and industrialism from their mythical and religious past, but who in their insecurity painfully want a resolution to "their chronic need to be rid of fear, something to meet the obscure needs of daily lives amidst strange and threatening facts."[65] Communism, like fascism, offers a new religion, a new myth; but Cross thinks that behind the propaganda for democracy and peace is a cynical plan of super minds, who, with their historical insights, promise a panacea out of their own passion to rule. However, Cross discovers that in assuming the role of arbiter of the future for such men as Hilton, Herndon, and Blount, he has become no better than they; for, as he learns, "if you fought men who tried to conquer you in terms of total power you too had to use total power and in the end you became what you tried to defeat."[66]

During his Party activities Cross becomes fascinated with Blount's wife, Eva, who serves to strengthen Wright's judgment on Cross's actions. An artist, she has been tricked into her marriage through a Party plot to wed her high social position and abundant finances to the Party through Gil Blount. Cross surreptitiously reads her diary and finds that she too is a rebel, an outsider. Her distraught state of mind is also reflected in her subjective, expressionistic paintings. An affair between the two develops, and for the first time Cross feels that love and communication between people are possible. However, their relationship is suddenly and sensationally terminated when Eva plunges from a window to her death, after she has learned of Cross's hideous history. With "one swift look into the black depths of his heart, into the horror of his deeds," she chooses death over life with a monster.[67] Cross is made to pay a penalty for his acts—to be stranded without love. The responsibility that he has undertaken for his life is turned against him, and he is propelled deeper into a lonely existential darkness. A nihilistic-existential approach, Wright implies, carries its own chaotic and suicidal logical illogic, which, tragically, is the ultimate ambiguity of a philosophy dependent upon ambiguities.

The Outsider is proof not of Wright's existentialism but of his rejection of existentialism. In his portrayal of the destruction left in the path of a man who had walked outside history and society, Wright was really asking man to be responsible for others as well as for himself. Although in his nonfiction after *The Outsider* he found certain existential tenets useful, especially for exposing the myths he thought man often irrationally lived by, and although he may not have fully realized what he was doing philosophically in *The Outsider*, the direction of his thinking in the 1950s had shifted away from the grim and dark side of existentialism seen in "The Man Who Lived Underground." Wright's position recalls, in fact, one which a French Communist implied really lurks behind the existentialism of Sartre. In a public dialogue the Marxist Naville accused Sartre of "attempting to revive the essential nature of reformism, of humanistic liberalism, in a highly specific situation, namely, the present historical situation."[68] It is this humanistic, reformist attitude that Wright seems to have returned to in *The Outsider*.

Wright's late nonfiction confirms such an interpretation. It reveals rational and pragmatic premises, combined with a trust that man, if he would listen to his reason, could create relatively peaceful and secure societies that would permit the greatest possible dignity and freedom. And even though Wright's later novel, *The Long Dream*, has been attacked for protesting an American racial situation that by 1958 bore no resemblance to contemporary fact, the inspiration for Wright's protest was consistent with that for such diverse works as *Native Son* and *The Outsider*—that man's reason could discover a way out of a history of injustices and irrationalities. Finally, *Savage Holiday*, by exploring a chain of absurdities built upon the unwillingness of the main character to view rationally his motivations and his existence, underscores how reason should be the key to reality. In many ways it mirrors the approach taken by Wright more than twenty years before in his early short story, "Superstition."

Marxism at one time apparently provided for Wright the pseudo-scientific foundation for the construction of a rational and peaceful world. His later disillusionment with the Communist Party could possibly have influenced his writing of the pessimistic "The Man Who Lived Underground." However, *The Outsider* is a return to older concepts once held by Wright—feelings and ideas that really grew out of *Black Boy*. What scholar Kingsley Widmer thinks is the philosophical control behind *The Outsider* is, in fact, what Wright must essentially stand for: that the twentieth-century forces of industrialism and science, rather than alienating man from man, may be transformed into forces that are morally good; that some sort of ethical and social idealism may be propounded to discipline existence in the modern world; and that man, if he is capable of discovering and using idealism, must certainly, at the center, be benevolent.[69]

Wright's protests were shouted ones. He often painted grotesque pictures of compulsive violence and fragmented psyches. Yet underneath, he seems to have cherished a hope in, and a future for, man at his best. Wright no doubt realized that journeys through the labyrinth of the human mind and struggles against the injustices of history and societies would be treacherous, but they might ultimately be rewarding. However, his late nonfiction ominously expresses that time is quickly closing in on man. Wright wanted to be heard, not as a prophet of doom or as a messiah. He desperately hoped that he would not be a voice crying in the wilderness. Instead, he fervently wished that his words would educate his readers and inspire them to apply their reasons to building a rational world.

CHAPTER 5

New Directions?
A Postscript

THE UNEXPECTED DEATH of a writer in his middle age invites curiosity about new works that perhaps were being written by him near the time of his death. If fragments do exist and a late publication is different in subject or tone, scholars and critics will often theorize about a change in the philosophical direction or the aesthetic vision of the writer. Such speculation can prove flattering to the reputation of the dead author, because a critic is apt to discover more good in the promise than in the actual production. Wright did leave fragments of unpublished works. Taken together with a novel and a few late short works, including poetry, they are merely hints of fresh perspectives on his part. If, in fact, the last items and fragments do represent anything solid enough to signal changes and new trends, they suggest that Wright was: (1) turning some of his attentions away from man and society to nature, (2) renewing an earlier interest in writing poetry, (3) converting into fiction certain experiences and observations from his European life and from his foreign travels, (4) experimenting with drama or mass-media dramatic forms, and (5) for the first time endowing his works with touches of humor.

Except for brief instances in *Black Power* and *Pagan Spain,* Wright had never displayed an ability or a propensity to transform into words any evocations and impressions he might have received from natural beauty and phenomena. He apparently felt that he should focus his writing upon what he thought were the more important social and philosophical problems facing man. Even when he found it necessary to write physical descriptions, he usually concentrated on people and objects. Such portrayals are generally terse, journalistic, and non-metaphorical. However, near the end of his life, Wright was composing hokku and haiku poetry. Both of these Japanese forms consist of three unrhymed lines, normally of five, seven, and five syllables. Hokku is typically epigrammatic; haiku contains references to one of the seasons. Most of Wright's published late poetry is characterized by the latter.[1] Yet, in such short pieces nature could hardly be developed as a topic. The seasons are merely mentioned, and Wright's poems are often oriented around a picture image or thought outside of nature.[2] If his imagination did interact with the forces and beauties of nature, the results in his late poems seem perfunctory.

Before his death Wright did finish another novel, a sequel to *The Long Dream* set in France. He titled it *Island of Hallucination.* Only five episodes from that manuscript have ever been published, although Wright's biographer, Constance Webb, has sketched the remainder of the novel.[3] In one episode Fishbelly Tucker, the central character in *The Long Dream,* is chased in his first hours in Paris by a crowd who is after his colorful hat. Haunted by racially oriented thoughts from his American Southern past, Fishbelly must contend with the fear-instilling images arising from his memory. In a later episode, Fishbelly thoughtfully returns a set of false teeth lost by an old Frenchwoman. His reward is a slap in the face. He again is reminded of the South when he compares the woman's reaction, a result of her sense of shame, to his own experiences in the South, where he had been forced to feel shame "a million times . . . for things that one ought not be ashamed of, shame that made one even more ashamed when one realized that one was helpless to fight against it."[4] The remaining three episodes revolve around the stories of three Negro Americans in Paris. These tales are told to Fishbelly by a lawyer friend, Ned. One is about a brilliant law student at the Sorbonne who is afraid to return to the States. The last two sketches are of Negroes who are hardly admirable people. Irene Stout has made a small fortune in Paris by writing letters to American tourists telling them the sad tale of her woes as a Negro. Of course, the white Americans have responded generously out of guilt feelings that have followed them to Europe. Another Negro, Jimmy Whitfield, continues his scheme in Paris to sleep with young, white American girls and then to extort money from them for his silence to their parents.

Considered together, the five episodes are little more than a glimpse at a larger work that someday might have shed more light on Wright's life and thinking during his years in Europe. If anything, they reveal that Wright was willing to expose qualities in exiled Negroes that were not flattering. By so doing, he could still attack indirectly the American racial attitudes that had helped to form people such as Irene Stout and Jimmy Whitfield. As in most of his writing, he was making an appeal to men of reason, especially to whites, to correct those conditions causing absurdity to be heaped upon absurdity. In terms of artistic technique the episodes represent no radical departures in style or authorial viewpoint. Wright continued to employ the third-person, omniscient narrator, centering on Fishbelly's consciousness. The lawyer Ned, with his vignettes of other Negro Americans, is apparently not intended to be a foil to Fishbelly. He is a friend who will educate the younger Fishbelly to some of the ways of Negro expatriots in France. Although five episodes are hardly enough to indicate a significant metamorphosis by Wright, they do not seem embued with the sense of outrage, anger, and frustration characteristic of his early works.

Two radio scripts and a short story suggest that perhaps Wright was actually gravitating toward a spirit of comic irony. Even James Baldwin, in his remarks on the radio scripts, "Man of All Work" and "Man, God Ain't like That . . . ," detects "a new tone, . . . a less uncertain distance, and a new depth," and he applauds the humor that has entered the works.[5] The comedy of situation in "Man of All Work" has already been noted in Chapter 1 of this study. A potentially tragic conclusion is resolved without a sensational murder only after the white Mr. Fairchild has attempted a sexual assault on Carl, a Negro who is disguised as a woman. Like a British Restoration dramatist, Wright combines social satire with comic action based upon appearance and reality.

Much the same is done in a second radio script, "Man, God Ain't Like That . . ." Here, though, the satire is extended to the international scene. Besides offering a racial commentary, Wright attacks European Christianity for intruding into Africa and causing irreparable damage to black psychology. In Africa the American painter John and his recently acquired mistress, Elsie Franklin, decide to take back with them to Paris an ignorant but likable black native, Babu, who has derived from European missionaries a vague and distorted notion of Christianity. The plot hinges on the ironic reversal from an early statement made by John, "These savages think we're gods."[6] Later, Babu, dazed by the white man's civilization in Paris, disappears, carrying the bones of his dead father in a suitcase. In a few months he returns to John's apartment, claiming that he has searched for and found the true God. Babu's hazy notions about the Christian God have led him to believe that he must kill the true God in order to effect a resurrection and then a salvation for men, specifically for black men, so that they might have the fine buildings and modern conveniences that the white man obtained after the death of Christ. Having sought without success the white God in Paris—because for Babu "all white men look alike," another ironic twist of stereotyped racial attitudes— he has at last found a painting of God.[7] The painting turns out to be of John—another irony—who had earlier posed as Christ for other artists. Of course, Babu slays John and returns to Africa, presumably expecting to see technological miracles there. Meanwhile, the Paris police continue to track down suspects, having already dismissed Babu, because, after all, he has appeared to be a good and God-fearing Christian.

"Man, God Ain't Like That . . ." is thus a mixture of the serious, the comic, and the absurd. Bloodshed is not spared, as Babu hacks away at John in the process of beheading him. Behind the story seems to be an intelligence almost playfully humorous. Wright seems to be laughing, but not cynically, at the absurd travesties man has allowed himself to be a party to, if not the cause of. Like "Man of All Work," this radio script is a sign that Wright possessed some talent for working in dramatic genres to project tragically ironic materials into the area of the objectively comical.

Wright's last short story, "Big Black Good Man," also has a foreign setting, Copenhagen. Any of its comic success depends on a single irony. Old Olaf Jensen, a traveled seaman before his retirement, is a night porter in a hotel catering to sailors. Though he thinks that he has no racial prejudices, the rather diminutive Olaf feels frightened and threatened when he is confronted by a "too big, too black, too loud, too direct and probably too violent" American seaman who asks for service.[8] Olaf hesitantly allows the Negro to stay in the hotel and then makes genuine efforts to fulfill his needs for women and liquor. As the Negro is about to leave, he places his huge black hands around Olaf's neck, and Olaf is almost fatally stricken from fear. But the giant departs grinning, and Olaf swears revenge if he should ever return. Exactly a year later the black American enters the hotel, and, still grinning, he again places his hands around Olaf's neck. Just as Olaf is about to reach for a gun, the black man produces for him six beautiful nylon shirts, correct in their neck size. They are a gift to Olaf for the past services he had rendered. The supposedly murderous intentions of the Negro have been, after all, really an expression of his gratitude. Good race relations are restored; the Negro is as human as any white man; and Olaf discovers a friend in this "big black good man."

The tale needs no further explication to underline its triteness. It would suffer greatly from a comparison with any of the stories in *Uncle Tom's Children*, written two decades before. However, Wright's attempt to combine serious materials with ironic comedy is consistent with his two radio scripts. The three together then represent what may have been the beginning of a trend toward a comic vision.

Nothing in Wright's late works dissolves the thesis that his efforts were those of a black man who, even in his anger, fear, outrage, and frustration, was generally sounding his pleas for change to the ears and minds of rational men, especially white men. If anything, the last short pieces suggest that Wright, the man, was mellowing and that he now could occasionally smile. In fact, according to one of his Paris friends, the self-exiled native son was seriously contemplating just before he died a return to live in his native land.[9]

Had Wright lived beyond 1960, had he returned to America to witness its racial turbulence of the 1960s, and had he continued to be influenced by his rationalist humanism, he no doubt would have been an object of scornful attack from such black militants as Malcolm X, Stokely Carmichael, and LeRoi Jones. For them the days of protest had ended. The white man had not listened, and the black man himself now had to act. There could be no room for the likes of a Wright, "a white liberal's nigger." History had no more space for reason, when white man's logic could not see beyond black man's skin color.

But perhaps without men of protest like Wright, an age of black militancy could never have existed.

Notes

PREFACE

1. Harold R. Isaacs, *The New World of Negro Americans* (New York, 1963), p. 248.

2. John A. Williams, "Introduction," *White Man, Listen!* by Richard Wright (Garden City, N.Y., 1964), p. xi.

CHAPTER I: ON THE AMERICAN PRIMARY COLORS

1. Richard Wright, *Black Boy: A Record of Childhood and Youth* (New York, 1945), p. 228.

2. For instance, see Ralph Ellison, "Richard Wright's Blues," *Antioch Review*, V (Summer 1945), 198–199. This article is reprinted in Ellison's *Shadow and Act* (New York, 1964), pp. 77–94.

3. Rebecca C. Barton, *Witnesses for Freedom: Negro Americans in Autobiography* (New York, 1948), p. 255.

4. From Constance Webb's biography, *Richard Wright: A Biography* (New York, 1968), we learn that Wright wanted *Black Boy* to be more than autobiographical. Webb says of

Wright that "he would use himself as a symbol of all the brutality and cruelty wreaked upon the black man by the Southern environment," p. 205.

5. Wright, *Black Boy*, p. 25.

6. Ralph K. White, "Black Boy: A Value-Analysis," *Journal of Abnormal and Social Psychology*, XLII (Oct. 1947), 440–461.

7. Ibid., pp. 447–458.

8. Ibid., p. 449.

9. Wright, *Black Boy*, p. 3.

10. Ibid., p. 41.

11. Ibid., p. 65.

12. Ibid., p. 151.

13. Ibid., p. 172.

14. Ibid., p. 120; p. 33.

15. Ibid., p. 228.

16. Wright's "The Ethics of Living Jim Crow: An Autobiographical Sketch" was first published by the Federal Writers' Project in *American Stuff* (New York, 1937), pp. 39–52. It was reprinted in his *Uncle Tom's Children: Five Long Stories* (New York, 1938), an expanded version of *Uncle Tom's Children: Four Novellas* (New York, 1938).

17. The publication history of Wright's early short stories is complicated. The first, "Superstition," was printed in *Abbott's Monthly Magazine*, II (Apr. 1931), 45–47, 64–66, 72–73 (a discussion of this story appears in Chapter 4). "Big Boy Leaves Home" first appeared in *The New Caravan*, ed. Alfred Kreymborg et al. (New York, 1936), pp. 124–158, and was reprinted in both versions of *Uncle Tom's Children*. "Silt," in *New Masses*, XXIV (Aug. 24, 1937), 19–20, was included in Wright's *Eight Men* (Cleveland, 1961) as "The Man Who Saw the Flood." "Fire and Cloud," in both versions of *Uncle Tom's Children*, was published initially in *Story*, XII (Mar. 1938), 9–41. "Bright and Morning Star," in the expanded edition of *Uncle Tom's Children*, was first printed in *New Masses*, XXVII (May 10, 1938), 97–99, 116–124. Later in 1938 it was published in book form by International Publishers in New York. "Down by the Riverside" and "Long Black Song" appeared in both versions of *Uncle Tom's Children*.

18. Wright, *Uncle Tom's Children: Four Novellas*, p. 16.

19. Ibid., p. 58.

20. For a detailed account of this interpretation, see Edwin Berry Burgum, "The Art of Richard Wright's Short Stories," *Quarterly Review of Literature*, I (Spring 1944), 207–208.

21. Wright, *Uncle Tom's Children: Four Novellas*, p. 211.

22. Ibid., p. 178.

23. Richard Wright, *12 Million Black Voices: A Folk History of the Negro in the United States* (New York, 1941), p. 30.

24. Wright, *Uncle Tom's Children: Four Novellas*, p. 166.

25. Richard Wright, *Bright and Morning Star* (New York, 1938), p. 20. The International Publishers' edition has been used.

26. Wright, *Black Boy*, p. 219.

27. Wright, *12 Million Black Voices*, p. 100.

28. Ibid., p. 127.

29. The autobiographical sketches set in Chicago are an extension of *Black Boy* and provide a limited amount of information and background material for a reading of both *Lawd Today* and *Native Son*. The longest piece is "Early Days in Chicago," in *Cross Section 1945: A Collection of New American Writing*, ed. Edwin Seaver (New York, 1945), pp. 306–342. It appeared later in *Eight Men* as "The Man Who Went to Chicago." Some of the same material is found in "American Hunger," *Mademoiselle*, XXI (Sept. 1945), 164–165, 299–301; also in "What You Don't Know Won't Hurt You: A Belated Report on the Progress of Medical Research," *Harper's Magazine*, CLXXXVI (Dec. 1942), 58–61. Wright's account of his participation in the Communist Party in Chicago was first printed in two parts as "I Tried to Be a Communist," *Atlantic Monthly*, CLXXIV (Aug. 1944), 61–70; (Sept. 1944), 48–56. It was republished without title in the more familiar *The God That Failed*, ed. Richard Crossman (New York, 1949), pp. 115–162.

30. See Nick Aaron Ford, rev. of *Lawd Today, CLA Journal*, VII (Mar. 1964), 270.

31. Wright, *Eight Men*, p. 215.

32. Richard Wright, *Lawd Today* (New York, 1963), p. 156.

33. Ibid., p. 103.

34. Ibid., p. 114.

35. Ibid., p. 101.

36. Ibid., p. 103.

37. Wright, *12 Million Black Voices*, p. 128.

38. The importance of *Native Son* in the history of Negro literature has been noted by too many critics and scholars to mention here. However, the following are particularly useful: Hugh M. Gloster, *Negro Voices in American Fiction* (Chapel Hill, N.C., 1948); Carl Milton Hughes, *The Negro Novelist: A Discussion of the Writings of American Negro Novelists 1940–1950* (New York, 1953); Robert A. Bone, *The Negro Novel in America* (New Haven, 1958); and David Littlejohn, *Black on White: A Critical Survey of Writing by American Negroes* (New York, 1966). Received too late for consideration in this study were two recent books on Wright: Edward Margolies, *The Art of Richard Wright* (Carbondale, Ill., 1969), and Dan McCall, *The Example of Richard Wright* (New York, 1969).

39. See Bone, *Negro Novel*, pp. 153–166, for a lengthy account of the "Wright School of Protest." A revised edition of Bone's book, published in 1965, adds a section on James Baldwin but changes none of the material on Wright or the novelists in the "Wright School of Protest."

40. James Baldwin, *Notes of a Native Son* (Boston, 1955), p. 31.

41. For instance, see David L. Cohn, "The Negro Novel: Richard Wright," *Atlantic Monthly*, CLXV (May 1940), 659–661; and Burton Rascoe, "Negro Novel and White Reviewers," *American Mercury*, L (May 1940), 113–117.

42. See Richard Wright, "I Bite the Hand That Feeds Me," *Atlantic Monthly*, CLXV (June 1940), 828. Wright's article is a direct response to Cohn's review.

43. Baldwin, *Notes of a Native Son*, p. 38.

44. Richard Wright, *Native Son* (New York, 1940), p. 8.

45. Baldwin, *Notes of a Native Son*, p. 35.

46. Richard Wright, *How "Bigger" Was Born: The Story of Native Son, One of the Most Significant Novels of Our Time, and How It Came to Be Written* (New York, 1940), p. 10.

47. Wright, *Native Son*, p. 14.

48. Ibid., p. 17.

49. Baldwin, *Notes of a Native Son*, pp. 33–34.

50. Wright, *Native Son*, p. 9.

51. Ibid., p. 204.

52. An analysis of the elemental symbols employed by Wright appears in Harry Slochower, *No Voice is Wholly Lost . . . : Writers and Thinkers in War and Peace* (New York, 1945), pp. 87–92.

53. Wright, *Native Son*, p. 203.

54. An idea expressed by Bone, *Negro Novel*, p. 145.

55. Wright, *Native Son*, p. 345.

56. Wright, "I Bite the Hand," p. 828.

57. Wright, *Native Son*, p. 91.

58. Ibid., p. 97.

59. Ibid., p. 247.

60. Ibid., p. 333.

61. Ibid., p. 339.

62. Wright, *How "Bigger" Was Born*, pp. 29–30.

63. Richard Wright, "Is America Solving Its Race Problem?" *Negro Digest*, III (Aug. 1945), 44.

64. James Baldwin, *Nobody Knows My Name: More Notes of a Native Son* (New York, 1961), p. 188.

65. This story by Wright was first published as "Almos' A Man" in *Harper's Bazaar*, no. 2732 (Jan. 1940), pp. 40–41, 105–107.

66. Wright, *Eight Men*, p. 193. This story was reprinted from *Zero*, I (Spring 1949), 45–53.

67. Wright, *Eight Men*, pp. 193–194.

68. Baldwin, *Nobody Knows My Name*, pp. 182–183.

69. Suggested by Baldwin in *Nobody Knows My Name*, p. 186.

70. Journalist and cartoonist Ollie Harrington, one of Wright's friends in Paris, indicates that both "Man of All Work" and "Man, God Ain't Like That . . ." were written for a German radio network. See Harrington, "The Last Days of Richard Wright," *Ebony*, XVI (Feb. 1961), 94.

71. Granville Hicks, "The Power of Richard Wright," *Saturday Review*, XLI (Oct. 18, 1958), 13, 65.

72. Saunders Redding, "The Way It Was," *New York Times Book Review*, Oct. 26, 1958, p. 4.

73. Saunders Redding, "The Alien Land of Richard Wright," *Soon, One Morning: New Writing by American Negroes, 1940–1962*, ed. Herbert Hill (New York, 1963), pp. 58–59.

74. Richard Wright, *The Long Dream* (Garden City, N.Y., 1958), p. 253.

75. Ibid., p. 142. This idea seems to echo the grandfather's words in Ralph Ellison's *Invisible Man*.

76. Ibid., p. 157.

77. Ibid., p. 67. Fishbelly's observation also controls the dominant image in "The Man Who Killed a Shadow" in *Eight Men*.

78. Ibid., p. 383.

79. Baldwin, *Nobody Knows My Name*, p. 188.

80. Richard Wright, "Between the World and Me," *Partisan Review*, II (July–Aug. 1935), 18–19.

CHAPTER 2: MARXISM, THE PARTY, AND A NEGRO WRITER

1. Richard Wright, *Black Boy: A Record of Childhood and Youth* (New York, 1945), p. 17.

2. Wilson Record, *The Negro and the Communist Party* (Chapel Hill, N.C., 1951), p. 315. For a succinct summary of Record's study, consult his final chapter, " 'Red and Black: Unblending Colors,' " pp. 287–315.

3. Richard Wright, ["I Tried to Be a Communist"], *The God That Failed*, ed. Richard Crossman (New York, 1949), p. 116.

4. Ibid., p. 118.

5. Constance Webb, *Richard Wright: A Biography* (New York, 1968), p. 157.

6. See Webb, *Richard Wright*, p. 410, fn. 17.

7. Richard Wright, *Black Power: A Record of Reactions in a Land of Pathos* (New York, 1954), p. xi.

8. Wright, ["I Tried to Be a Communist"], pp. 145–146.

9. Ibid., pp. 144–146.

10. Wright's reaction was like that of many American literary figures. Some writers—for instance, John Dos Passos in his trilogy *U.S.A.* (1930–1936) and Norman Mailer in *Barbary Shore* (1951)—have turned the process into subject matter for their novels.

11. Richard Wright, "Exchange of Letters," *Twice A Year*, XII (Spring–Summer 1945), 261.

12. Wright, *Black Power*, pp. xi–xii.

13. "Red Clay Blues," the last of these poems, was composed in collaboration with Langston Hughes. It appeared in *New Masses*, XXXII (Aug. 1, 1939), 14.

14. Wright, ["I Tried to Be a Communist"], p. 120.

15. The poems appeared together in *Left Front*, I (Jan.–Feb. 1934), 3.

16. Richard Wright, "Strength," *The Anvil*, no. 5 (Mar.–Apr. 1934), p. 20.

17. Richard Wright, "Everywhere Burning Waters Rise," *Left Front*, no. 4 (May–June 1934), p. 9.

18. Richard Wright, "Child of the Dead and Forgotten Gods," *The Anvil*, no. 5 (Mar.–Apr. 1934), p. 30.

19. Richard Wright, "I Have Seen Black Hands," *New Masses*, XI (June 26, 1934), 16.

20. Richard Wright, "Ah Feels It in Mah Bones," *International Literature*, no. 4 (Apr. 1935), p. 80.

21. Richard Wright, "Red Leaves of Red Books," *New Masses*, XV (Apr. 30, 1935), 6.

22. Richard Wright, "Spread Your Sunrise!" *New Masses*, XVI (July 2, 1935), 26.

23. Richard Wright, "We of the Streets," *New Masses*, XXIII (Apr. 13, 1937), 14.

24. Richard Wright, "Old Habit and New Love," *New Masses*, XXI (Dec. 15, 1936), 29.

25. Richard Wright, "Transcontinental," *International Literature*, V (Jan. 1936), 52–57.

26. For an account of this incident, see Wright, ["I Tried to Be a Communist"], pp. 159–162.

27. An observation made by Walter B. Rideout in *The Radical Novel in the United States 1900–1954: Some Interrelations of Literature and Society* (Cambridge, Mass., 1956), p. 260.

28. See Edwin Berry Burgum, "The Art of Richard Wright's Short Stories," *Quarterly Review of Literature*, I (Spring 1944), 207–208.

29. Richard Wright, *Uncle Tom's Children: Four Novellas* (New York, 1938), p. 173.

30. Ibid., p. 259.

31. Ibid., p. 301.

32. Richard Wright, *Bright and Morning Star* (New York, 1938), p. 3.

33. Ibid., p. 26.

34. Ibid., p. 48.

35. Richard Wright, "Blueprint for Negro Writing," *The New Challenge*, II (Fall 1937), 60.

36. Ibid., p. 63.

37. Richard Wright, *12 Million Black Voices: A Folk History of the Negro in the United States* (New York, 1941), p. 10.

38. Ibid., p. 35.

39. Ibid., p. 12.

40. Ibid., pp. 145–146.

41. Ibid., pp. 122–123.

42. Richard Wright, *Lawd Today* (New York, 1963), p. 28.

43. Ibid., p. 32.

44. Ibid., p. 54.

45. Ibid., p. 58.

46. Ibid., p. 150.

47. Ibid., p. 158. The train image may have been suggested by the Communist expression, "the locomotive of history."

48. Richard Wright, *Native Son* (New York, 1940), p. 28.

49. Ibid., p. 57.

50. Ibid., p. 98.

51. Ibid., pp. 326–327.

52. See fn. 41 for Chapter 1 for a full citation of Cohn's review article.

53. Richard Wright, "I Bite the Hand That Feeds Me," *Atlantic Monthly*, CLXV (June 1940), 826–827. An interesting, though unrelated, twist is that soon after the public exchange of differences between Wright and Cohn, Wright married an American Jew.

54. Robert A. Bone makes this point in *The Negro Novel in America* (New Haven, 1958), p. 150.

55. Some critics have debated the extent to which Cross Damon's race is related to the theme of alienation. For a view maintaining that Cross's attitudes are basically derived from racial factors, see Morris Beja, "It Must Be Important: Negroes in Contemporary American Fiction," *Antioch Review*, XXIV (Fall 1964), 323–336. For an opposing view, consult Arthur P. Davis, " 'The Outsider' as a Novel of Race," *Midwest Journal*, VII (Winter 1956), 320–326; or Nick Aaron Ford, "Four

Popular Negro Novelists," *Phylon*, XV (First Quarter 1954), 29–39.

56. Richard Wright, "Introduction," *Black Metropolis: A Study of Negro Life in a Northern City*, by Horace R. Cayton and St. Clair Drake (New York, 1945), p. xxix.

57. Richard Wright, *The Outsider* (New York, 1953), pp. 324–338.

58. Webb, *Richard Wright*, p. 157.

CHAPTER 3: NEW PERSPECTIVES OUTSIDE AMERICA

1. For an extended account of the specific circumstances and incidents that probably influenced Wright in this respect, see Constance Webb, *Richard Wright: A Biography* (New York, 1968), pp. 242–262.

2. In 1949 Wright stopped in Chicago for a few days, after being filmed on an Argentine location in the role of Bigger Thomas in a movie version of *Native Son*. A portion of the film was shot in Chicago's South Side slums. There he apparently was forced to bribe policemen in order to carry on the film-making. He also had trouble in obtaining hotel accommodations in Chicago. These experiences and Wright's reactions to them are recorded in "The Shame of Chicago," *Ebony*, VII (Dec. 1951), 24–32. Wright's comments drew a sharp attack from one of the editors of *Ebony* in the same issue; for this article see Ben Burns, "Return of the Native Son," p. 100. For a pictorial story about the film version of *Native Son*, see " 'Native Son' Filmed in Argentina," *Ebony*, VI (Jan. 1951), 82–86. This article also contains a brief description of Wright's life in Paris.

3. Richard Wright, *Black Power: A Record of Reactions in a Land of Pathos* (New York, 1954), pp. 3–5.

4. Ibid., pp. xiii–xiv.

5. Harold R. Isaacs, *The New World of Negro Americans* (New York, 1963), p. 253.

6. Wright, *Black Power*, p. iii.

7. Ibid., p. 104.

8. Ibid., pp. 321–324.

9. Ibid., p. 91.

10. Ibid., p. 346.

11. Ibid., pp. 342–349.

12. Ibid., p. 345.

13. Richard Wright, *Lawd Today* (New York, 1963), p. 95.

14. Richard Wright, *12 Million Black Voices: A Folk History of the Negro in the United States* (New York, 1941), p. 146.

15. Wright, *Black Power*, p. 28.

16. Ibid., p. 175.

17. Ibid., pp. 196–197.

18. Isaacs, *New World*, pp. 253–254.

19. Wright, *Black Power,* p. 342.

20. Richard Wright, *The Color Curtain: A Report on the Bandung Conference* (Cleveland, 1956), pp. 11–15.

21. Ibid., p. 15.

22. Isaacs, *New World*, p. 249.

23. Wright, *The Color Curtain*, p. 74.

24. Ibid., pp. 157–160.

25. Ibid., pp. 162–163.

26. Ibid., pp. 220–221.

27. Ibid., pp. 216–217.

28. Ibid., p. 219.

29. Ibid., pp. 220–221.

30. Ibid., p. 219.

31. Ibid., p. 203.

32. Ibid., p. 115.

33. Ibid., p. 193.

34. The occasions and the cities (Rome, Hamburg, Paris, Stockholm, etc.) are mentioned briefly in "Why and Wherefore," Wright's introduction to *White Man, Listen!* (Garden City, N.Y., 1957), pp. 15–16. Although Wright says that some of the lectures were delivered as early as 1950, it is apparent, because of his insertion of materials easily dated 1954 at the earliest, that the manuscripts for his lectures underwent revision for publication. From James Baldwin we learn that the second section of *White Man, Listen!* is derived from a Paris speech that Wright delivered on Sept. 21, 1956, at the Conference of Negro-African Writers and Artists. For Baldwin's remarks and his reactions to Wright's speech, see *Nobody Knows My Name:*

More Notes of a Native Son (New York, 1961), pp. 44–47.

35. Wright, *White Man, Listen!* p. 34.

36. Ibid., pp. 78–79.

37. Ibid., pp. 97–98.

38. Ibid., p. 7. Sharing a place on the dedication page is Eric Williams, chief minister of Trinidad and Tobago, whom Wright calls "my friend."

39. Ibid., pp. 80–82.

40. Ibid., pp. 100–101.

41. Ibid.

42. Ibid., p. 52.

43. Ibid., pp. 72–73.

44. Ibid., pp. 141–142.

45. Ibid., p. 147.

46. Ibid., p. 115.

47. Ibid., pp. 149–150.

48. Richard Wright, *Pagan Spain* (New York, 1957), pp. 1–2.

49. For two additional sketches of Spanish life by Wright, about prostitutes and youthful pimps, see "Spanish Snapshots," *Two Cities*, no. 2 (July 15, 1959), pp. 25–34.

50. Wright, *Pagan Spain*, pp. 151–152.

51. Ibid., p. 186.

52. Ibid., pp. 64–66.

53. Ibid., p. 193.

54. Ibid., pp. 93–114. Wright's description of the bullfight ranks as one of his most emotionally forceful and pictorially vivid accounts of a real event. Its tone, its sensitivity to undercurrents of passion within a crowd, and its terse but concise language recalls a much earlier piece, Wright's report of the jubilant reaction of Chicago Negroes to boxer Joe Louis's victory over Max Baer in Sept. 1935. For this article, see "Joe Louis Uncovers Dynamite," *New Masses*, XVII (Oct. 8, 1935), 18–19.

55. Wright, *Pagan Spain*, p. 99.

56. Ibid., pp. 134–135.

57. Ibid., pp. 192–193.

58. Ibid., pp. 203–204.

59. Ibid., p. 195.

60. Ibid., p. 192.

CHAPTER 4: THE PHILOSOPHICAL PREMISES

1. Wright refers to these men in various autobiographical pieces, in his nonfiction, and in many epigraphs. In *The Outsider*, Cross Damon, the main character, is familiar with most of them. For a list of authors read by Cross, see *The Outsider* (New York, 1953), p. 388.

2. In *Existentialism and Alienation in American Literature* (New York, 1965), Sidney Finkelstein treats, among other things, the essential differences between Marxism and existentialism in their respective approaches to history. See especially pp. 11–135. Among the figures he examines are Marx, Kierkegaard, Nietzsche, Husserl, Heidegger, Jaspers, Camus, and Sartre.

3. Wright's interest in Mencken is revealed in *Black Boy: A Record of Childhood and Youth* (New York, 1945), pp. 217–218. He alludes to Mencken's *A Book of Prefaces* and *Prejudices*. Wright also mentions three-dozen or so other writers to whom Mencken had referred and whom Wright himself says he wants to know more about, including Nietzsche and Dostoyevsky. By the late 1930s, according to the novelist-essayist Ralph Ellison, Wright was familiar with many of Dostoyevsky's works. See Ellison's *Shadow and Act* (New York, 1964), p. 15.

4. Wright, *Black Boy*, pp. 97–98.

5. Ibid., pp. 71–72.

6. Ibid., p. 89.

7. Ibid., pp. 87–88. Note here a relationship between Wright's confession and certain modes of existential thought.

8. Ibid., p. 100.

9. Richard Wright, *12 Million Black Voices: A Folk History of the Negro in the United States* (New York, 1941), pp. 17–18.

10. Ibid., pp. 131–136.

11. Richard Wright, *Lawd Today* (New York, 1963), p. 143.

12. "Superstition" actually was not the first story published by Wright. In *Black Boy* he says that when he was fifteen (around 1924), a Jackson, Miss., newspaper, *Southern Register*, printed "The Voodoo of Hell's Half-Acre" in three install-

ments. Wright calls the story "crudely atmospheric, emotional, intuitively psychological." Its plot is about "a villain who wanted a widow's home." For Wright's remarks about the story and its publication, consult *Black Boy*, pp. 144–147. Attempts to locate a copy of "The Voodoo of Hell's Half-Acre" have been futile.

13. Richard Wright, "Superstition," *Abbott's Monthly Magazine*, II (Apr. 1931), 73.

14. Richard Wright, *Uncle Tom's Children: Four Novellas* (New York, 1938), p. 301.

15. Nathan A. Scott, Jr., "Search for Beliefs: Fiction of Richard Wright," *University of Kansas City Review*, XXIII (Winter 1956), 135, fn. 8.

16. Two publishers have printed *Savage Holiday* in paperbound editions. Between lurid covers Avon Publications in New York issued the novel in 1954. Ten years later, reprint rights were acquired by Award Books in New York, and its edition was released in Mar. 1965.

17. Richard Wright, *White Man, Listen!* (Garden City, N.Y., 1957), pp. 87–91.

18. Ibid., p. 89.

19. Richard Wright, *Savage Holiday* (New York, 1965), p. 9.

20. Ibid., p. 21.

21. Ibid., p. 38.

22. Ibid., p. 105.

23. Ibid., p. 134.

24. Ibid., p. 183.

25. Ibid., p. 216.

26. William Gardner Smith does claim that "there was something very American . . . about his basic Puritanism." The remark appears in "Richard Wright (1908–1960): The Compensation for the Wound," *Two Cities*, no. 6 (Summer 1961), p. 67.

27. See Scott, "Search for Beliefs," especially p. 132. A discussion of the existential undertones in Wright's early fiction appears in Irving Howe, "Black Boys and Native Sons," *Dissent*, X (Autumn 1963), 353–368. The article also appears in Howe's *A World More Attractive: A View of Modern Literature and Politics* (New York, 1963), pp. 98–122.

28. Richard Wright, *How "Bigger" Was Born* (New York, 1940), p. 10.

29. Richard Wright, *Native Son* (New York, 1940), p. 9.

30. Ibid., pp. 90–94.

31. Ibid., p. 252.

32. Ibid., p. 37.

33. Ibid., p. 204.

34. Ibid., pp. 301–302.

35. Ibid., p. 228.

36. "The Man Who Lived Underground" first appeared in full in *Cross-Section: A Collection of New American Writing,* ed. Edwin Seaver (New York, 1944), pp. 58–102. Wright had probably worked out this long tale earlier, for in 1942 he published two excerpts later included in the story. See "The Man Who Lived Underground: Two Excerpts from a Novel," *Accent,* II (Spring 1942), 170–176. The completed story was included in *Eight Men,* a collection published posthumously. Certain scenes in the story resemble parts of Ellison's *Invisible Man.*

37. Howe, "Black Boys," p. 365.

38. Saunders Redding, "Richard Wright's Posthumous Stories," rev. of *Eight Men, New York Herald Tribune Book Review,* Jan. 22, 1961, p. 33.

39. Herbert Hill, ed., "Introduction," *Soon, One Morning: New Writing by American Negroes, 1940–1962* (New York, 1963), p. 8.

40. Richard Wright, *Eight Men* (Cleveland, 1961), p. 64.

41. Ibid., p. 75.

42. Ibid., p. 59.

43. Ibid., p. 92.

44. Wright, *Black Boy,* p. 33. The word *not* in the last sentence of the passage is indeed used ambiguously. However, because of the context from which the passage has been removed and of the parenthetical nature of the remark itself, an interpretation leaning toward a pessimistically motivated intention on the part of Wright seems plausible.

45. Saunders Redding, "The Alien Land of Richard Wright," *Soon, One Morning,* p. 58. Redding also immediately points out that what was good for Wright as "a social being was bad for his work," because, Redding feels, Wright was too far away in time and space from the States to provide an ac-

curate picture of the American racial scene in such late works as *The Long Dream.*

46. Such criticisms are found, for example, in the following: Nick Aaron Ford, "Four Popular Negro Novelists," *Phylon,* XV (First Quarter, 1954), 29–39; Phoebe Adams, "The Wrong Road," rev. of *The Outsider, Atlantic Monthly,* CLXLI (May 1953), 77–78; Steven Marcus, "The American Negro in Search of Identity," *Commentary,* XVI (Nov. 1953), 456–463.

47. Discussions of the existential theme in *The Outsider* are found in the following: Richard Lehan, "Existentialism in Recent American Fiction: The Demonic Quest," *Texas Studies in Literature and Language,* I (Summer 1959), 181–202; and Kingsley Widmer, "The Existentialist Darkness: Richard Wright's *The Outsider,*" *Wisconsin Studies in Contemporary Literature,* I (Fall 1960), 13–21.

48. Wright, *The Outsider,* p. 125.

49. *Ibid.,* p. 405.

50. Lehan, "Existentialism," pp. 193–194.

51. Morris Beja, "It Must Be Important: Negroes in Contemporary American Fiction," *Antioch Review,* XXIV (Fall 1964), 330.

52. Widmer, "Existentialist Darkness," p. 17.

53. Wright, *The Outsider,* p. 8.

54. Ibid., p. 25.

55. Ibid., p. 347.

56. Ibid., p. 16.

57. Ibid., p. 80.

58. Ibid., p. 83.

59. Ibid., p. 110.

60. Ibid., p. 114.

61. Ibid., p. 127.

62. Ibid., p. 404.

63. Ibid.

64. Ibid., p. 345.

65. Ibid., p. 330.

66. Ibid., p. 225.

67. Ibid., p. 372.

68. Jean-Paul Sartre, *Existentialism,* trans. Bernard Frechtman (New York, 1947), pp. 70–85.

69. Widmer, "Existentialist Darkness," p. 14.

CHAPTER 5: NEW DIRECTIONS?
A POSTSCRIPT

1. About a dozen of these poems have been published. One source claims that Wright composed about four thousand of them. See Constance Webb, *Richard Wright: A Biography* (New York, 1968), p. 393.

2. These poems are found in Ollie Harrington, "The Last Days of Richard Wright," *Ebony*, XVI (Feb. 1961), 92. Harrington published six of them and called them "Hai-Kai Poems." These six and two more, all called "Hokku Poems," are also found in *American Negro Poetry*, ed. Arna Bontemps (New York, 1963), pp. 104–105. Four others appear in Webb, *Richard Wright*, pp. 393–394.

3. Wright apparently developed nothing more from his 1940 comment in *How "Bigger" Was Born* (New York, 1940) that he was "launching upon another novel, this time about the status of women in modern American society," p. 38. Horace Cayton reveals that before going to Paris, Wright had been talking to him about a different story he was working on. The main figure was to be a Negro woman, who was almost light skinned enough to pass as a white but who, in her attempts to look white, was unknowingly using a bleaching cream containing arsenic. Thus, as Cayton suggests, she was committing both sociological and biological suicide. For Cayton's remarks, see "A Symposium on an Exiled Native Son," *Anger, and Beyond: The Negro Writer in the United States*, ed. Herbert Hill (New York, 1966), p. 210. Wright apparently had other plans for fictional works; but in the last five years of his life they were either frustrated or interrupted by his travels away from France, by the nonfiction that developed from those trips, and, also, by his work on *The Long Dream*. Constance Webb tells us that in 1955 Wright was outlining a series of novels that "would cut across racial, class, sexual, religious and political questions." Each volume, according to Webb, "would stand on its own and yet its highest significance would be found in the context of an evocative, impersonal mood which would be sustained throughout several volumes." Both poetry and prose were to be combined in these novels. One novel was to be a companion piece to *Savage Holiday*. Tentatively entitled *A Strange Daughter*, it was to feature a repressed, white,

Episcopalian girl and an African. Another novel, *When the World Was Red*, was to be about the king of the Aztecs: "Montezuma's intellect would embrace the God of the Spaniards but their wanton murders would force his emotions and spirit to reject Christianity." Another plot was to grow out of a Whitmanesque poem Wright had composed. For this poem and other remarks about Wright's plans and hopes for future creative activities, see Webb, *Richard Wright*, pp. 356–357.

4. Richard Wright, "Five Episodes from an Unfinished Novel," *Soon, One Morning: New Writing by American Negroes, 1940–1962*, ed. Herbert Hill (New York, 1963), p. 149.

5. James Baldwin, *Nobody Knows My Name: More Notes of a Native Son* (New York, 1961), pp. 182–183.

6. Richard Wright, *Eight Men* (Cleveland, 1961), p. 164.

7. Ibid., p. 188.

8. Ibid., pp. 96–97. "Big Black Good Man" first appeared in *Esquire*, XLVIII (Nov. 1957), 74–80.

9. Cayton, "Exiled Native Son," p. 206.

Selected Bibliography

WORKS BY RICHARD WRIGHT

Novels

Lawd Today. New York: Walker & Co., 1963.
The Long Dream. Garden City, N.Y.: Doubleday & Co., 1958.
Native Son. New York: Harper & Bros., 1940.
The Outsider. New York: Harper & Bros., 1953.
Savage Holiday. New York: Universal Publishing and Distributing Corp., 1965.

Short Fiction and Short-Fiction Collections

Bright and Morning Star. New York: International Publishers, 1938.
Eight Men. Cleveland: World, 1961.
"Five Episodes from an Unfinished Novel," *Soon, One Morning: New Writing by American Negroes, 1940–1962*, ed. Herbert Hill. New York: Alfred A. Knopf, 1963, pp. 140–164.
"The Man Who Lived Underground," *Cross-Section: A Collection of New American Writing*, ed. Edwin Seaver. New York: L. B. Fischer, 1944, pp. 58–102.
"The Man Who Lived Underground: Two Excerpts from a Novel," *Accent*, II (Spring 1942), 170–176.

"Superstition," *Abbott's Monthly Magazine*, II (Apr. 1931), 45–47, 64–66, 72–73.

Uncle Tom's Children: Five Long Stories. New York: Harp. & Bros., 1938.

Uncle Tom's Children: Four Novellas. New York: Harper & Bros., 1938.

Poetry

"Ah Feels It in Mah Bones," *International Literature*, no. 4 (Apr. 1935), p. 80.

"Between the World and Me," *Partisan Review*, II (July–Aug. 1935), 18–19.

"Child of the Dead and Forgotten Gods," *The Anvil*, no. 5 (Mar.–Apr. 1934), p. 30.

"Everywhere Burning Waters Rise," *Left Front*, no. 4 (May–June 1934), p. 9.

"Hai-Kai Poems," "The Last Days of Richard Wright," by Ollie Harrington, *Ebony*, XVI (Feb. 1961), 92.

"Haiku Poems," *Richard Wright: A Biography*, by Constance Webb. New York: G. P. Putnam's Sons, 1968, pp. 393–394.

"Hearst Headline Blues," *New Masses*, XIX (May 12, 1936), 14.

"Hokku Poems," *American Negro Poetry*, ed. Arna Bontemps. New York: Hill & Wang, 1963, pp. 104–105.

"I Am a Red Slogan," *International Literature*, no. 4 (Apr. 1935), p. 35.

"I Have Seen Black Hands," *New Masses*, XI (June 26, 1934), 16.

"Old Habit and New Love," *New Masses*, XXI (Dec. 15, 1936), 29.

"Red Clay Blues," *New Masses*, XXXII (Aug. 1, 1939), 14. (With Langston Hughes.)

"Red Leaves of Red Books," *New Masses*, XV (Apr. 30, 1935), 6.

"A Red Love Note," *Left Front*, I (Jan.–Feb. 1934), 3.

"Rest for the Weary," *Left Front*, I (Jan.–Feb. 1934), 3.

"Spread Your Sunrise!" *New Masses*, XVI (July 2, 1935), 26.

"Strength," *The Anvil*, no. 5 (Mar.–Apr. 1934), p. 20.

"Transcontinental," *International Literature*, V (Jan. 1936), 52–57.

"We of the Streets," *New Masses*, XXIII (Apr. 13, 1937), 14.

Nonfiction and Autobiographical Books and Articles

"American Hunger," *Mademoiselle*, XXI (Sept. 1945), 164–165, 299–301.

Black Boy: A Record of Childhood and Youth. New York: Harper & Bros., 1945.

Black Power: A Record of Reactions in a Land of Pathos. New York: Harper & Bros., 1954.

"Blueprint for Negro Writing," *The New Challenge*, II (Fall 1937), 53–65.

The Color Curtain: A Report on the Bandung Conference. Cleveland: World, 1956.

"Early Days in Chicago," *Cross Section 1945: A Collection of New American Writing*, ed. Edwin Seaver. New York: L. B. Fischer, 1945, pp. 306–342.

"The Ethics of Living Jim Crow: An Autobiographical Sketch," *American Stuff: An Anthology of Prose & Verse by Members of the Federal Writers' Project, with Sixteen Prints by the Federal Art Project.* New York: Viking Press, 1937, pp. 39–52.

"Exchange of Letters," *Twice A Year*, XII (Spring–Summer 1945), 255–261. (With Antonio R. Frasconi.)

How "Bigger" Was Born: The Story of Native Son, One of the Most Significant Novels of Our Time, and How It Came to Be Written. New York: Harper & Bros., 1940.

"I Bite the Hand That Feeds Me," *Atlantic Monthly*, CLXV (June 1940), 826–828.

["I Tried to Be a Communist"], *The God That Failed*, ed. Richard Crossman. New York: Harper & Bros., 1949, pp. 115–162.

"Introduction," *Black Metropolis: A Study of Negro Life in a Northern City*, by Horace R. Cayton and St. Clair Drake. New York: Harcourt, Brace, 1945, pp. xvii–xxxiv.

"Is America Solving Its Race Problem?" *Negro Digest*, III (Aug. 1945), 42–44.

"Joe Louis Uncovers Dynamite," *New Masses*, XVII (Oct. 8, 1935), 18–19.

Pagan Spain. New York: Harper & Bros., 1957.

"Rascoe-Baiting," *American Mercury*, L (July 1940), 376–377.

"The Shame of Chicago," *Ebony*, VII (Dec. 1951), 24–32.

"Spanish Snapshots," *Two Cities*, no. 2 (July 15, 1959), pp. 25–34.

12 Million Black Voices: A Folk History of the Negro in the United States. New York: Viking Press, 1941. (With Edwin Rosskam, photo-director.)

"What You Don't Know Won't Hurt You: A Belated Report on the Progress of Medical Research," *Harper's Magazine*, CLXXXVI (Dec. 1942), 58–61.

White Man, Listen! Garden City, N.Y.: Doubleday & Co., 1957.

SECONDARY SOURCES

Adams, Phoebe. "The Wrong Road," rev. of *The Outsider*, by Richard Wright, *Atlantic Monthly*, CLXLI (May 1953), 77–78.

Baldwin, James. *Nobody Knows My Name: More Notes of a Native Son*. New York: Dial Press, 1961.

Baldwin, James. *Notes of a Native Son*. Boston: Beacon Press, 1955.

Barton, Rebecca Chalmer. *Witnesses for Freedom: Negro Americans in Autobiography*. New York: Harper & Bros., 1948.

Beja, Morris. "It Must Be Important: Negroes in Contemporary American Fiction," *Antioch Review*, XXIV (Fall 1964), 323–336.

Bone, Robert A. *The Negro Novel in America*, 2d. ed. New Haven: Yale University Press, 1965.

Brown, Deming Bronson. *Soviet Attitudes Toward American Writing*. Princeton: Princeton University Press, 1962.

Bryer, Jackson R. "Richard Wright (1908–1960): A Selected Checklist of Criticism," *Wisconsin Studies in Contemporary Literature*, I (Fall 1960), 22–33.

Burgum, Edwin Berry. "The Art of Richard Wright's Short Stories," *Quarterly Review of Literature*, I (Spring 1944), 198–211.

Burgum, Edwin Berry. "The Promise of Democracy and the Fiction of Richard Wright," *Science and Society*, VII (Fall 1943), 338–352.

Burns, Ben. "Return of the Native Son," *Ebony*, VII (Dec. 1951), 100.

Cleaver, Eldridge. *Soul on Ice*. New York: McGraw-Hill, 1967.

Cohn, David L. "The Negro Novel: Richard Wright," *Atlantic Monthly*, CLXV (May 1940), 659–661.

Cruse, Harold. *The Crisis of the Negro Intellectual*. New York: William Morrow & Co., 1967.

Davis, Arthur P. " 'The Outsider' as a Novel of Race," *Midwest Journal*, VII (Winter 1956), 320–326.

Ellison, Ralph. "Richard Wright's Blues," *Antioch Review*, V (Summer 1945), 198–211.

Ellison, Ralph. *Shadow and Act*. New York: Random House, 1964.

Embree, Edwin R. *13 Against the Odds*. New York: Viking Press, 1944.

Fabre, Michael, and Edward Margolies, "Richard Wright (1908–1960): A Bibliography," *Bulletin of Bibliography*, XXIV (Jan.–Apr. 1965), 131–133, 137.

Finkelstein, Sidney. *Existentialism and Alienation in American Literature*. New York: International Publishers, 1965.

Ford, Nick Aaron. "Four Popular Negro Novelists," *Phylon*, XV (First Quarter 1954), 29–39.

Ford, Nick Aaron. "The Ordeal of Richard Wright," *College English*, XV (Oct. 1953), 87–94.

Ford, Nick Aaron. Rev. of *Lawd Today*, by Richard Wright, *CLA Journal*, VII (Mar. 1964), 269–270.

French, Warren. *The Social Novel at the End of an Era*. Carbondale: Southern Illinois University Press, 1966.

Glicksberg, Charles I. "Existentialism in *The Outsider*," *Four Quarters*, VII (Jan. 1958), 17–26.

Glicksberg, Charles I. "Negro Fiction in America," *South Atlantic Quarterly*, XLV (Oct. 1946), 477–488.

Gloster, Hugh M. *Negro Voices in American Fiction*. Chapel Hill: University of North Carolina Press, 1948.

Hand, Clifford. "The Struggle to Create Life in the Fiction of Richard Wright," *The Thirties: Fiction, Poetry, Drama*, ed. Warren French. DeLand, Fla.: Everett Edwards, 1967.

Harrington, Ollie. "The Last Days of Richard Wright," *Ebony*, XVI (Feb. 1961), 83–94.

Hicks, Granville. "The Power of Richard Wright," rev. of *The Long Dream*, by Richard Wright, *Saturday Review*, XLI (Oct. 18, 1958), 13, 65.

Hill, Herbert, ed. *Anger, and Beyond: The Negro Writer in the United States*. New York: Harper & Row, 1966.

Hill, Herbert, ed. *Soon, One Morning: New Writing by American Negroes, 1940–1962*. New York: Alfred A. Knopf, 1963.

Howe, Irving. "Black Boys and Native Sons," *Dissent*, X (Autumn 1963), 353–368.

Hughes, Carl Milton. *The Negro Novelist: A Discussion of the Writings of American Negro Novelists 1940–1950*. New York: Citadel Press, 1953.

Isaacs, Harold R. *The New World of Negro Americans*. New York: John Day, 1963.

Jackson, Blyden. "The Negro's Image of the Universe as Reflected in His Fiction," *CLA Journal*, IV (Sept. 1960), 22–31.

Knox, George. "The Negro Novelist's Sensibility and the Outsider Theme," *Western Humanities Review*, XI (Spring 1957), 137–148.

Lehan, Richard. "Existentialism in Recent American Fiction: The Demonic Quest," *Texas Studies in Literature and Language*, I (Summer 1959), 181–202.

Littlejohn, David. *Black on White: A Critical Survey of Writing by American Negroes*. New York: Grossman Publishers, 1966.

McCall, Dan. *The Example of Richard Wright*. New York: Harcourt, Brace & World, 1969.

Marcus, Steven. "The American Negro in Search of Identity," *Commentary*, XVI (Nov. 1953), 456–463.

Margolies, Edward. *The Art of Richard Wright*. Carbondale: Southern Illinois University Press, 1969.

Margolies, Edward. *Native Sons: A Critical Study of Twentieth Century Negro American Authors*. Philadelphia: J. B. Lippincott, 1968.

Mendelson, Moris Osipovich. *Soviet Interpretation of Contemporary American Literature*, trans. Deming B. Brown and Rufus W. Mathewson. Washington: Public Affairs Press, 1948.

" 'Native Son' Filmed in Argentina," *Ebony*, VI (Jan. 1951), 82–86.

Owens, William A. "Introduction," *Native Son*, by Richard Wright. New York: Harper & Bros., 1957, pp. vii–xii.

Rascoe, Burton. "Negro Novel and White Reviewers," *American Mercury*, L (May 1940), 113–117.

Record, Wilson. *The Negro and the Communist Party*. Chapel Hill: University of North Carolina Press, 1951.

Redding, J. Saunders. "Richard Wright's Posthumous Stories," rev. of *Eight Men*, by Richard Wright, *New York Herald Tribune Book Review*, Jan. 22, 1961, p. 33.

Redding, J. Saunders. "The Way It Was," rev. of *The Long Dream*, by Richard Wright, *New York Times Book Review*, Oct. 26, 1958, p. 4, 38.

Rideout, Walter B. *The Radical Novel in the United States 1900–1954: Some Interrelations of Literature and Society*. Cambridge: Harvard University Press, 1956.

Riesman, David. "Marginality, Conformity, and Insight," *Phylon*, XIV (Third Quarter 1953), 241–257.

Sartre, Jean-Paul. *Existentialism*, trans. Bernard Frechtman. New York: Philosophical Library, 1947.

Sartre, Jean-Paul. *What Is Literature?* trans. Bernard Frechtman. New York: Philosophical Library, 1949.

Scott, Nathan A., Jr. "The Dark and Haunted Tower of Richard Wright," *Comment* (Wayne State University), VII (July 1964), 93–99.

Scott, Nathan A., Jr. "Judgment Marked by a Cellar: The American Negro Writer and the Dialectic of Despair," *The Shapeless God: Essays on Modern Fiction*, ed. Harry J. Mooney, Jr., and Thomas F. Staley. Pittsburgh: University of Pittsburgh Press, 1968, pp. 139–169.

Scott, Nathan A., Jr. "Search for Beliefs: Fiction of Richard Wright," *University of Kansas City Review*, XXIII (Autumn 1956), 19–24; (Winter 1956), 131–138.

Silberman, Charles E. *Crisis in Black and White*. New York: Random House, 1964.

Slochower, Harry. *No Voice Is Wholly Lost . . . : Writers and Thinkers in War and Peace*. New York: Creative Age Press, 1945.

Smith, William Gardner. "Black Boy in France," *Ebony*, VIII (July 1953), 32–36, 39–42.

Smith, William Gardner. "Richard Wright (1908–1960): The Compensation for the Wound," *Two Cities*, no. 6 (Summer 1961), pp. 67–69.

Sullivan, Richard. "Afterword," *Native Son*, by Richard Wright. New York: New American Library of World Literature, 1961, pp. 394–399.

Webb, Constance. *Richard Wright: A Biography*. New York: G. P. Putnam's Sons, 1968.

White, Ralph K. "Black Boy: A Value-Analysis," *Journal of Abnormal and Social Psychology*, XLII (Oct. 1947), 440–461.

Widmer, Kingsley. "The Existential Darkness: Richard Wright's *The Outsider*," *Wisconsin Studies in Contemporary Literature*, I (Fall 1960), 13–21.

Williams, John A. "Introduction," *White Man, Listen!* by Richard Wright. Garden City, N.Y.: Doubleday & Co., 1964, pp. ix–xii.

Winslow, Henry F. "Richard Nathaniel Wright: Destroyer and Preserver (1908–1960)," *The Crisis*, LXIX (Mar. 1962), 149–163, 187.

Index

"Ah Feels It in Mah Bones," 57
Antichrist, The (Friedrich Nietzsche), 135–136
Anvil, The (journal), 55
Atlantic Monthly, 52

Baldwin, James, 30, 31, 32, 33, 39–40, 41, 42, 48, 111, 124, 169
Barton, Rebecca C., 5
Beja, Morris, 157
"Between the World and Me," 48
"Big Black Good Man," 170–171. *See also Eight Men*
"Big Boy Leaves Home," 14–15, 16. *See also Uncle Tom's Children: Four Novellas*
Black Boy, ix, 4–11, 13, 15, 19, 21, 25, 28, 30, 32, 33, 37, 40, 43, 45, 47, 50, 122, 124–127, 148, 153–154, 164
Black Power, 88, 90–100, 102, 104, 105, 106, 107, 110, 112, 118, 119, 167
"Bright and Morning Star," 13, 19, 20, 62, 63–66, 132, 133, 153. *See also Uncle Tom's Children: Five Long Stories*

Calvin, John, 134
Camus, Albert, 120, 155
Carmichael, Stokely, 172
Cayton, Horace R., 188n
"Child of the Dead and Forgotten Gods," 56
Chou En-lai, 102–103, 104
Cohn, David L., 81
Color Curtain, The, 88, 100–106, 107, 110, 112, 118, 119
Communist Party, xi, 13, 29, 52–92 *passim,* 100, 101, 103, 104, 121, 122, 123, 130, 148, 154, 164

Daily Worker, The (Party organ), 53
"Dead, The" (James Joyce), 66
Dos Passos, John, 29, 178n
Dostoyevsky, Feodor, 124, 148, 149, 158, 184n
"Down by the Riverside," 17–19, 61. *See also Uncle Tom's Children: Four Novellas*

Dreiser, Theodore, 21
Dumas, Alexandre, 111

Eight Men, x, 14, 39–42, 60, 121, 123, 124, 143–144, 148–154, 163, 164, 169–171
Ellison, Ralph, 83, 111, 149, 150, 178*n,* 186*n*
Engels, Friedrich, 51, 52, 120
"Ethics of Living Jim Crow, The," 4, 11–13
"Everywhere Burning Waters Rise," 56

Farrell, James Thomas, 29
"Fire and Cloud," 13, 19–20, 57, 62–63, 132–133. *See also Uncle Tom's Children: Four Novellas*
"Five Episodes from an Unfinished Novel," 167–169
Formación Politica, 114
Franco, Francisco, 113, 114
Frasconi, Antonio R., 54
Freud, Sigmund, 120, 123, 133, 134, 136, 137, 139, 140, 141, 142, 143

God That Failed, The (Richard Crossman, ed.), 52, 53, 54, 55, 83
Go Tell It on the Mountain (James Baldwin), 124

Hegel, Georg W. F., 50, 120, 127
Heidegger, Martin, 120, 158
Hicks, Granville, 43
Hill, Herbert, 149, 150
Himes, Chester, 111
How "Bigger" Was Born, 32
Howe, Irving, 149
Hughes, Langston, 179*n*
Husserl, Edmund, 120

"I Have Seen Black Hands," 56–57

International Publishers, 63
Invisible Man (Ralph Ellison), 83, 149, 150, 178*n,* 186*n*
Isaacs, Harold R., xii, 99, 101
Island of Hallucination, 167–169
"I Tried to Be a Communist," 52, 53, 54, 55, 83

Jaspers, Karl, 120
John Reed Club, 13, 51–52
Jones, LeRoi, 30, 172
Joyce, James, 5, 66

Kierkegaard, Sören, 120, 123

Lawd Today, 22–28, 29, 31, 35, 36, 70, 71–77, 78, 80, 81, 82, 98, 129–131, 132, 158
Left Front (journal), 51, 55
Lenin, Nikolai, 120
Lewis, Sinclair, 21
"Long Black Song," 13–14, 16–17, 35, 60, 61–62. *See also Uncle Tom's Children: Four Novellas*
Long Dream, The, xi, 39, 42–48, 86, 164, 167
Luther, Martin, 134

Mailer, Norman, 178*n*
Malcolm X, 172
"Man, God Ain't Like That . . . ," 169–170. *See also Eight Men*
"Man of All Work," 41–42, 169, 170. *See also Eight Men*
"Man Who Killed a Shadow, The," 40–41. *See also Eight Men*
"Man Who Lived Underground, The," x, 39, 121, 123, 124, 143–144, 148–154, 163, 164. *See also Eight Men*
"Man Who Saw the Flood, The." *See Eight Men;* "Silt"
"Man Who Was Almost a Man,

The," 40, 41. *See also Eight Men*

Marxism, *passim. See also* Communist Party

Marx, Karl, 50, 51, 52, 54, 93, 120, 127, 133

Mencken, Henry Louis, 123, 184*n*

Nasser, Gamal Abdel, 109

Native Son, ix, x, xi, 4, 21, 22, 23, 28–39, 41, 42, 53, 70, 71, 77–82, 85, 90, 94, 121, 123, 128, 143, 144–148, 149, 153, 154, 158, 164

Naville, M., 163

Nehru, Jawaharlal, 102, 109

Nietzsche, Friedrich, 120, 123, 124, 126, 133, 135–136, 137, 143, 148, 151, 155, 158, 159, 160, 161, 184*n*

Nkrumah, Kwame, 90, 94, 95, 96, 97, 99, 104, 109

"Old Habit and New Love," 58

Outsider, The, x, xi, 33, 82–85, 88, 90, 95, 121–122, 123, 124, 128, 143, 144, 149, 153, 155–164

Pagan Spain, 88, 112–119, 135, 167

Passos, John Dos. *See* Dos Passos, John

Pushkin, Alexander, 111

Record, Wilson, 51

Redding, J. Saunders, 43, 149

"Red Leaves of Red Books," 57–58

"Red Love Note, A," 56

"Rest for the Weary," 56

Roosevelt, Franklin D., 72

Sartre, Jean-Paul, 87, 120, 124, 126, 155, 163

Savage Holiday, 86, 123, 133–143, 164

"Silt," 14, 60. *See also Eight Men*

"Spread Your Sunrise!" 57–58

Steinbeck, John, 29

Strange Daughter, A, 188*n*–189*n*

"Strength," 56

Sukarno, Achmed, 109

"Superstition," 59–60, 131–132, 164

Thus Spake Zarathustra (Friedrich Nietzsche), 136

Totem and Taboo (Sigmund Freud), 136

"Transcontinental," 58–59

Trotsky, Leon, 54

12 Million Black Voices, 17, 38, 53, 56, 66–71, 72, 92, 98, 128–129, 130

Twilight of the Idols (Friedrich Nietzsche), 135–136

Uncle Tom's Children: Five Long Stories, x, 13–21, 35, 39, 53, 57, 60–66, 132–133, 153, 171

Uncle Tom's Children: Four Novellas, x, 13–21, 39, 53, 57, 60–63, 132–133, 171

"Voodoo of Hell's Half-Acre, The," 184*n*–185*n*

Washington, Booker T., 75

Webb, Constance, 52, 53, 143, 167

"We of the Streets," 58

Wheatley, Phillis, 111

When the World Was Red, 189*n*

White, Ralph K., 6–7

White Man, Listen! 106–112, 118, 119, 134–135

Widmer, Kingsley, 164

Williams, Eric, 183*n*

Williams, John A., xii

Yerby, Frank, 111

CRITICAL ESSAYS IN MODERN LITERATURE

William Faulkner: An Estimate of His Contributions to the Modern American Novel
by Mary Cooper Robb

The Fiction of John O'Hara
by E. Russell Carson

The Fiction and Criticism of Katherine Anne Porter (Revised)
by Harry J. Mooney, Jr.

The Hero in Hemingway's Short Stories
by Joseph DeFalco

Entrances to Dylan Thomas' Poetry
by Ralph Maud

James Gould Cozzens: Novelist of Intellect
by Harry J. Mooney, Jr.

Joyce Cary: The Comedy of Freedom
by Charles G. Hoffmann

The Short Stories of Ambrose Bierce
by Stuart C. Woodruff

The Fiction of J. D. Salinger (Revised)
by Frederick L. Gwynn and Joseph L. Blotner

The Novels of Anthony Powell
by Robert K. Morris

James Agee: Promise and Fulfillment
by Kenneth Seib

Richard Wright: An Introduction to the Man and His Works
by Russell Carl Brignano